Three Months in Mao's China

T0335001

Three Months in Mao's China

Between the Great Leap Forward and
the Cultural Revolution

Erik Zürcher

Edited by Erik-Jan Zürcher and Kim van der Zouw

AUP

Originally published as: Erik Jan Zürcher, Kim van der Zouw (red.), *Het Verre Oosten. Oog in oog met het China van Mao* [ISBN 978 94 6298 050 1], Amsterdam University Press, 2016

Translation: Vivien Collingwood

Cover design: Sander Pinkse Boekproductie
Lay out: Crius Group, Hulshout

ISBN	978 94 6298 181 2
e-ISBN	978 90 4853 157 8 (pdf)
e-ISBN	978 90 4853 158 5 (ePub)
NUR	508 | 692

© E.-J. Zürcher, H. van der Zouw / Amsterdam University Press B.V., Amsterdam 2017

All rights reserved. No part of this publication may be reproduced, stored in a retrieval system or disclosed in any form or by any means (electronic, mechanical, photocopying, recording or otherwise) without the prior written permission of the publisher.

For Emma and Otto
In memory of their grandparents

Contents

Introduction

On 13 September 1964 my father, Erik Zürcher, turned 36. That year, his birthday was not celebrated during the day with the family, with coffee and cake and heated discussion as was customary, but in the evening, with a large party at a big house belonging to some married friends, Kitty and San Go.[1] It was a party with friends and colleagues, most of them linked to the Institute of Sinology in Leiden. There was drinking (a lot of drinking), and there was music, dancing and speeches. The dancing in particular was exceptional for this group of friends, for whom parties tended to mean drinking, smoking and endless chatting.

The reason for all this exuberance was that the birthday party was also a farewell party: two days later, together with his old college friend, Gan Tjiang-Tek,[2] the curator of the Chinese collection at the National Museum of Ethnology in Leiden, Erik would leave on a six-month voyage, of which four months, he hoped, would be spent in China.

By 1964, Erik Zürcher had been a professor in Leiden for three years. He was a 'sinologist'; that is to say, he had studied Chinese language and literature and had also taken his doctorate in that field in 1959. Despite this, it was not as Professor of Chinese that he was appointed in 1961. Leiden already had a professor in that field – Anthony ('Toon' to his friends) Hulsewé – and with just a handful of students of Chinese each year, two professors would have been too

---

1   Go Lam-san: a pharmacist in Leiden and family friend of Erik's.
2   Gan Tjiang-Tek was born in Bandung in 1919 and came to study in the Netherlands shortly after the Second World War. He became a Dutch citizen in 1963. Tek would remain lifelong friends with Erik and Henny and attended both their cremations.

much of a good thing. Erik had been a brilliant student though, and his thesis, *The Buddhist Conquest of China*, on which he had worked for six years, was recognized as a pioneering work immediately upon publication. Armed with offers from various American universities, he was able to set his terms. Leiden wanted to keep him, so in 1960 he was made a lector (a now-defunct university rank under that of professor), and less than a year later, in 1961, professor of 'the history of East Asia, and in particular East-West relations.' This somewhat bizarre title allowed the university to appoint him alongside Hulsewé, who was eighteen years his senior.[3] In any case, the post was well matched to Erik's interests. His thesis was on the way in which Buddhism (originally from India) had spread within China and the changes it had undergone in the process, and in later life he would become extremely interested in the history of the early Catholic mission in China, particularly in the Jesuits. Both are examples of contact between different cultures, with the underlying (comparative) question being why Buddhism, but not Christianity, became a national religion in China.

Erik very nearly missed out on becoming a sinologist at all. He had come to Leiden to study Egyptology, and made a start on this programme. That he became a sinologist was the doing of the same Tek who would become his travelling companion in 1964. During the initiation rituals at the Leiden University students' society, Tek (who was already a senior student) discovered Erik hiding behind the coats in the cloakroom. Rather than give him away, Tek began to

---

3   For more on the history of sinology in the Netherlands and Leiden, see W.L. Idema (ed.), *Chinese Studies in the Netherlands: Past, Present and Future*, Leiden: Brill, 2014.

persuade Erik of the advantages of studying Chinese. Some time later, Erik did indeed change programmes.

Erik had already been away from home for long periods prior to 1964. After graduating, in 1952 he had been 'lent out' by his tutor, the celebrated Leiden Sinologist J.J.L. Duyvendak (Hulsewé's predecessor),[4] to a Swedish colleague, the elderly art historian Osvald Sirén. That was how it used to be; the relationship between a professor and his students, assistants and doctoral students was a cross between a guild-like master-apprentice relationship and a form of serfdom. The proposal by the brilliant but very authoritarian Duyvendak that Erik should move to Stockholm for six months was literally an offer that Erik couldn't refuse.

This can't have been easy, because in addition to graduating, Erik had also recently got married to someone who does not address us directly in this book, but who is nevertheless a central figure: my mother, Henny Dineke Bulten. It is typical of the academic relations of the time that Erik also asked, and received, Duyvendak's permission to marry. Although Henny would follow him to Sweden after a few months, this would be the first occasion – so soon after their marriage – on which she remained at home alone, as a sacrifice to academia. While working on his thesis, Erik moved once more, this time to Paris for a few months, to be supervised by Paul Demiéville, an eminent French Buddhologist and friend of Duyvendak's. Since 1956 Leiden had also had its own Professor of Buddhology, Jan de Jong, but for reasons that are no longer clear, Erik harboured a deep-rooted dislike of this man. He probably felt that De

4   J. (Jan) J.L. Duyvendak (1889-1954). He was appointed in Leiden in 1919 after working for years as an interpreter/translator at the Dutch Embassy in Beijing. He was a prominent figure in the Dutch academic world, including as rector of Leiden University.

Jong did not want to help him, out of a sense of rivalry. So off he went to Paris, which meant that Henny – now with a baby son – had to stay behind in Oegstgeest.

Although travelling for prolonged periods for study or work was nothing new, the journey to China in September 1964 was of a different order. After six years of university study, six years of doctoral research and three years as a professor, Erik had never once set foot in China. Nowadays this would be inconceivable; every student of Chinese spends a year, or even longer, in China. China is the world's fourth most popular tourist destination (with 55 million visitors a year) and large numbers of business travellers are constantly flying to and fro. The situation in 1964 was very different, however: in an age when only the jet set flew, and most people were only familiar with the inside of a jet plane from films, China was extremely far away. There were no direct flight connections between the Netherlands and China. The train took ten days and the boat at least three weeks.

China had always been a far-off land, of course; the expression 'the Far East' (also beloved of Chinese-East-Indian restaurants, perhaps for its nostalgic undertones) did not appear out of the blue. But at the time when Erik was studying and embarking on his academic career, it was further away than it had been for many years. Before the Second World War, there had been intensive trade relations and a great deal of missionary activity. Moreover, the Chinese community in the Dutch East Indies, which amounted to more than a million people, ensured constant contact with the Netherlands. All of this ended with the outbreak of war. In the years immediately following the war, China descended into a bloody civil war. In 1949, when Erik was in his third year at university, Mao Zedong's Communist

Party seized power. This was less traumatic for the Dutch than for the British and the Americans, with their considerable interests in China (moreover, the Netherlands was already deeply entangled in postcolonial wars in Indonesia, in which Erik's older half-brother Jan fought). However, the outbreak of the Korean War in 1950 brought an end to all relations. The Netherlands immediately followed its NATO ally, the United States, in branding North Korea an aggressor, and Dutch volunteers, including Erik's future colleague, the professor of Japanese Frits Vos (also present at the farewell party in 1964) went off to fight in Korea. From that time China was not only very far away, but also completely sealed off – at least, as far as Westerners were concerned. Any reports about the country that did emerge were largely based on rumour and speculation, which could lead to both massive exaggeration (of the threat posed by China) and grave under-estimation (of the numbers that died in the great famine). Erik and Tek's visit was therefore quite exceptional. They were able to go because the journey had an 'official' character. Erik had two objectives: for the Netherlands Organization for the Advancement of Pure Research (the ZWO, the predecessor of today's Netherlands Organization for Scientific Research, or NWO), he was to make an inventory of Chinese Research institutes and to research opportunities for collaboration; and for Leiden University, he was to research possibilities for student exchanges, and in particular possibilities for students of Chinese at Leiden to spend time in China. Tek was tasked with purchasing traditional folk-cultural objects for the museum. The journey was prepared in detail, and from beginning to end the reins were in the hands of the Chinese state travel agency, Luxingshe, which determined who could travel where and when.

With hindsight, we can see that Erik and Tek visited China during a 'window of opportunity'. The People's Republic had existed for fifteen years (they would watch the largest celebration of its founding). The country was recovering not only from the horrors of the Japanese occupation and the civil war, but also from what has ironically gone down in history as 'the Great Leap Forwards.'

In 1958, a radical wing within the leadership of the Communist Party led by Mao Zedong, contrary to the wishes of moderates such as Liu Shaoqi, Zhou Enlai and Deng Xiaoping, had forced through a large-scale programme of economic reform that was in fact a Chinese version of the collectivization and industrialization that Stalin had implemented in the Soviet Union in the 1930s. The goal was the same: to industrialize the country at a rapid pace. The state would fund the industrialization with the profits that would be made from the state monopoly on trade in agricultural produce. By buying grain and rice cheaply from farmers and selling them to town-dwellers and internationally at a higher price, the state would raise the money for factories, dams, railways and ships. As it was anticipated that the farmers, who made up the overwhelming majority of the Chinese population, would resist the reforms, agriculture was collectivized: small privately-owned farms and small cooperatives were forced to form large communes, which were put under party supervision. One of the most utopian aspects of Mao's campaign was that small farmers were tasked with building small blast furnaces and using them to produce their own iron, by melting down every available metal object, including surplus cooking pans, into raw material for industry.

Between 1958 and 1961, the Great Leap Forward swept the country like a destructive tornado. It led to an economic and human catastrophe, and one of the largest famines in Chinese and world history. There is much debate about the number of victims, but estimates range from 23 million to 45 million deaths. In the meantime, during the whole era of the Great Leap, China continued to export grain on a large scale in order to earn foreign currency for industrialization!

From 1960, resistance to Mao's politics grew within the party. At the 1962 party congress Mao was openly criticized and forced to perform public 'self-criticism'. Although he maintained his position as chairman of the party, he was so discredited that he had to relinquish the daily leadership. Mao remained the ultimate symbol of the Chinese revolution, but it was 'moderates' such as Liu Shaoqi, Deng Xiaoping and Zhou Enlai who ran the China that Erik and Tek visited in the autumn of 1964. Only two years after their visit, in 1966, Mao would stake everything, launch the 'Great Proletarian Cultural Revolution', regain power and eliminate his competitors.

In other words: our travellers' visit to China coincided with a breathing space that opened up between 1962 and 1966, when the country was not at the mercy of the megalomaniacal schemes of dogmatic ideologists. This certainly explains Erik's relatively positive assessment of the situation in China and the communist system. Despite – or, perhaps, because of – growing up in a communist family, he was certainly no communist himself, but at this time he was still a 'leftist' in a general sense: fiercely anti-colonial, quite anti-American, and burdened with a kind of equivocal aversion to the bourgeois circles in which he, a professor in Leiden, naturally moved.

His positive assessment also stemmed in part from a slightly Orientalist or paternalist attitude: 'We [Westerners] would not be able to live in such a system', he wrote in his diary, 'but for them [the Chinese] it is the only way'. At the same time, Erik was critical of the never-ending, all-permeating propaganda and indoctrination; clearly more critical, in any case, than Tek, who closely identified with the 'new China' and whom Erik saw as somewhat naïve. They had heated and sometimes vitriolic debates about this, but their friendship could take it.

For a long time, it was unclear as to how long Erik and Tek would be permitted to stay in China. In the end, they would stay for three months. On Christmas Eve they crossed the border into what was then British Hong Kong. They spent some time together in Hong Kong, but then their ways parted: Tek went to his family in Indonesia, Erik to Japan. From there, he travelled back to the Netherlands via India, Egypt (where my mother and I joined him), Turkey and Greece.

Throughout the journey to and around China, Erik faithfully kept a diary. In addition, each week, mostly on Sundays, he wrote a detailed letter to Henny in Oegstgeest (bits of which were read out to me). He had bought a modern Fujica single-lens reflex camera for the trip, and used it to take hundreds of photographs, or slides, to be accurate. Slides were extremely fashionable in the Netherlands in the early 1960s. While it seems strange looking back in 2015, at that time it was completely acceptable to invite one's friends and neighbours over for an evening, serve wine and cheese, and bore them with slides of your experiences for hours on end. Slides would come to play a central role in Erik's work. In the 1970s and 1980s he built up a picture archive of more than 20,000 slides (mostly photographs from books and journals). From 1991 this would form the basis of the 'China vision' project. At the end of the 1990s, the slide project was overtaken by the digital revolution, and under Erik's successors, it became of the earliest examples of digitalization in university education.

The slides that Erik took in China failed to withstand the ravages of time (or what was in fact fifty years of storage in the damp Warmond polder). The diary and the letters did survive, however, and they are the sources on which this short book is based. In 1964 Erik wrote in his diary: 'Puck[5] is keeping all my letters. That will be nice for later.' More than fifty years later, in early 2015, this did indeed prove to be the case.

Erik Zürcher remained a professor in Leiden until 1993. He became the best-known China specialist in the Netherlands, and enjoyed a special bond with the royal family from the late 1970s. He continued to work after his retirement in 1993, partly in increasingly small corners at the institute where he had been director, and partly at home in the large, secluded house in Warmond. It was there that he died, after a few final years troubled by health problems and increasing blindness, in February 2008. He was 79. Henny remained alone in the large house, feeling not the slightest need to dispose of Erik's things. Everything remained as it was, aside from his academic books, which were donated to the university library in Leuven (Erik had felt most akin to the kind of research that was done there).

At the beginning of 2015, when Henny herself passed away at the age of 87, almost exactly seven years after

---

5   For reasons that are no longer known, Henny's parents began calling her 'Puck' when she was a young. Erik kept the custom going. He spoke to others of her as Henny, but he called her Puck. As the letters show, her pet name for him was 'Eerft'.

Erik, Kim and I found his suits and ties still in the closets, his coats (still with their rolls of peppermints in the pockets) on the hallstand, and countless drawers full of paper throughout the whole house. We found them in the middle drawer of my mother's writing desk: fourteen airmail envelopes with Chinese stamps, large and red as propaganda posters, and in every envelope, three light-blue sheets of India-paper, crammed to the edges with my father's characteristically tiny but very readable handwriting.

For Kim and myself, the following weeks and months were an exhausting orgy of packing, clearing out, throwing away and passing on things, something that naturally entailed a continuous confrontation with the past lives of Erik and Henny, as well as with my own childhood. Weeks after discovering the letters in the writing desk, in my father's desk I came across an old exercise book with a hard, black-green cover. On reading the first sentences, it immediately became clear that this was a travel diary, the one that Erik had kept during the same journey to China in 1964. Two documents on the same subject, kept separately by two people for fifty years, had been reunited. The idea of publishing them as one came to us on the spot. After all, although these were very personal documents, they also had features that might make them interesting to others: they were uncensored reports on what was at that time a hermetically sealed country, written by an observer who was not merely a tourist or business traveller, but a professional trained China expert who was familiar with the language and kept his eyes and ears open.

When we first read the letters and the journal, it was clear that this was indeed an interesting historical source. In places, the text read like a message from another planet or

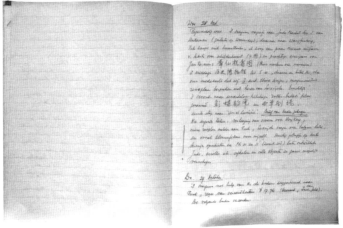

The travel journal.

something out of a time capsule; mostly due to the complete
metamorphosis that China has undergone since, but also
because of the glimpse that reading the texts allows into
the manners and way of life of the Dutch in the 1960s; and,
of course, due to the sometimes archaic spelling and choice

of words.[6] To cite J.P. Hartley's famous opening sentence, it is true that 'The past is a foreign country, and they do things differently there'.[7] At the same time, the text is so personal that those who knew Erik would immediately be able to recognize his voice without any trouble at all – it is as though one can hear him speaking.

After Amsterdam University Press expressed an interest in publishing the texts, we wondered what form such a book might take. The material consists of two very different sets of source texts, of course. Erik wrote the diary entries for himself; they were intended as a souvenir and reminder, and are full of references in Chinese to people, institutions and ideas. The letters are composed pieces of writing that were intended to keep the home front up to date, but also evidently to entertain. Sometimes the two sources complement one another, sometimes they overlap, and in some places they go in completely different directions.

Kim and I decided to make the letters the basis for the book. We present the letters in their entirety, with the exception of a few passages that relate solely to Henny's activities in Oegstgeest and Leiden and that do not relate in any way to the voyage to China. We include excerpts from the diary that complement the letters, either because they cover something that is not addressed in the letters, or because, on the contrary, they clarify a passage in the letters. After we had compiled a first rough draft of the manuscript, Erik's former colleague Wilt Idema, an emeritus professor in Leiden and Harvard, helped us enormously by providing expert advice on the meaning and spelling of the numerous

---

6   We have modernized the transcription of Chinese names and terms. Erik used the then common Wade-Giles transcription method, whereas we have used the Pinyin transcription method, which is more commonly used today.

7   J.P. Hartley, *The Go-between* (London: Hamish Hamilton, 1953, p. 1).

Chinese names, terms and places, something for which we remain extremely grateful. We are also grateful to the Leiden sinologist and art historian Oliver Moore, who was able to dig out many details of the objects that Tek and Erik brought back for the National Museum of Ethnology and themselves, and who helped us to navigate the catalogue of the museum.

We did not change the order of the texts in order to create 'storylines', but this does not mean that we cannot distinguish certain leitmotifs or themes that appear time and again in the letters and diary entries.

The most striking storyline is that of the old and the new China. Through his studies, Erik was mainly familiar with China from books. The first visit to the real, living China was thus a non-stop voyage of discovery, in which he continuously reflected on the question of the extent to which the old, classical, imperial China still lived on, and the extent to which the communist regime had fundamentally changed the country.

In order to be able to answer this question and understand China better, Erik and Tek worked long hours, certainly in the beginning, immersing themselves in both elite and mass culture. Night after night, they would visit film and theatrical performances, especially those of Peking opera in its classical and modernized forms; and they went to temples and palaces and toured the most important museums. Besides this, during the day they would visit working-class neighbourhoods with their performing storytellers, puppet theatres, singers and jugglers. This was aided by the fact that Tek had the task of purchasing traditional artefacts for Leiden's National Museum of Ethnology, which automatically took them to the markets and shopping districts where folk art was to be found. There, they also found the traditional Chinese cultural product *par excellence*: food. They ate at 300-year-old gourmet restaurants and at market taverns, and Erik diligently noted down everything he consumed. Luxingshe ensured that the achievements of modern China – in the form of factories, laboratories and agricultural communes – also got a place on the programme.

Whereas Tek's work took him to markets, Erik's work – exploring possibilities for academic collaboration and student exchanges – inevitably brought him into contact with the many layers of the enormous Chinese state and party bureaucracy. This results in a second storyline. Particularly in the diary, Erik frequently refers to the endless, lengthy discussions and negotiations. Although there was some interest within the bureaucracy at this time in intensifying collaboration with the West, Erik mostly came away from these discussions with a feeling of uncertainty. The same was true of the constant negotiations with the state tourism agency about the journey and the length of their stay (whether it would be two, three, or four months; whether they would go to the interior or not...). Both the positive and the negative decisions seem to have been completely unpredictable, and there is a great sense of being subject to an arbitrary will; which again led to constant speculation about China's motives.

A third storyline concerns the travellers' relationship with their own 'support network'. For Erik this was the Dutch Embassy, and in particular undersecretary Roland van den Berg. Van den Berg was a fellow sinologist who, like Erik, had studied in Leiden. In great contrast to Erik, however, he also had an insider's knowledge of China, because – having been born in Shanghai as the son of the Dutch consul – he had spent the first ten years of his life there.[8] Erik received a great deal of help from Van den Berg from the very start, something for which he was very grateful, but this did not deter him from making some barbed comments about the diplomatic world and Westerners in China in general in his letters and diary. The group that was most Tek's 'own' was that of the Dutch-East-Indian Chinese who had established themselves in China after the war, mainly as medical specialists, in the period when Tek himself had gone to the Netherlands. Meetings and discussions with these *huaqiao* ('overseas Chinese') were difficult, but also interesting, as this group – which the Chinese government considered to be essential, and who enjoyed special privileges – consisted of people who were both insiders and outsiders.

Finally, of course, the letters and the diary entries cover the human aspects that play a role in every journey, and certainly every long journey: illness and discomfort, annoyance at one's travelling companion (even though Erik and Tek actually made a very good team, all things considered) and homesickness. Homesickness was also a consequence of the degree of isolation that the travellers experienced in China, something that is utterly unimaginable for us. The Internet was still science fiction; there was no contact by telephone with the Netherlands; telegrams were for emergencies; letters took a week to arrive, on average; and foreign newspapers were not on sale. Erik and Tek knew very little of what was happening outside China – and even *in* China – and the news that they did receive had either been filtered by the Chinese party media or was subject to great delay. Meanwhile, things were happening in the outside

---

8   Roland van den Berg would later become the Dutch ambassador in Beijing. He would thus see how the student protests were suppressed violently in 1989 and how Queen Beatrix of the Netherlands' state visit was cancelled at the last minute (her household made it as far as the government plane on the runway at Schiphol).

world that autumn that the partygoers at the birthday party on 13 September would never have been able to imagine. It was known in advance that American presidential elections would be held and the Olympic Games would take place in Tokyo, but the deposition of Nikita Khrushchev as party leader in the Soviet Union and the detonation of the first Chinese atomic bomb came as a complete surprise. If there is one thing that the texts in this book make clear, it is how different the world was, fifty years ago; how far away, in other words, the Far East truly was.

From Moscow to Beijing

We know from the diary that Erik sent a first letter to Henny from Moscow, but this letter has not been preserved. In the following, we therefore describe the first days of the journey on the basis of the diary entries alone.

15 September
Journey went well. Tupolev[9] was cold and draughty, poor service, not to be repeated. In Moscow: Hotel Minsk, very modern and sterile. We were given an Intourist[10] voucher book for meals. NB. it proved to be fake! We ate a modest meal in the restaurant (*borscht + shashlik* plus a bottle of wine that turned out to be some kind of port) for 8.25 roubles (more than 32 guilders), equivalent to around half our entire voucher book! Keep a watch out for further foreign currency-milking. Tek used earplugs against my snoring, but proved to snore like a hurricane himself. Wrote a letter to Puck; went to bed quite early.

16 September
Had breakfast in the hotel using the vouchers (we cannot figure out the system). Saw the Kreml:[11] interesting icons, barbarous spectacle of colour and ornament. Visited Gum:[12]

---

9   Aeroflot, the airline of the Soviet Union, flew between Amsterdam and Moscow with a Tupolev 104, one of the world's first successful jet planes and in fact the only jet plane to be operational between 1956 and 1958.

10   The Soviet Union's state tourism agency. In both the Soviet Union and China at this time, foreigners could only take part in fully organized tours that had to be approved beforehand.

11   Strictly speaking, the more correct Russian term for what is commonly called the Kremlin.

12   The large department store on Moscow's Red Square, originally built in 1893.

abundance of wares, but of a poor quality and quite expensive. Lunched on sandwiches, standing in Gum. Bought a bottle of vodka (R. 3.45). We were picked up in the afternoon by Tichvinsky[13] and Yuri K., a boring and virtuously-diligent ethnologist who showed us around the Oriental Institute (old junk, dilapidated building, ca. 100.000 volumes, founded six years ago) and had dinner with us. Finally, visited the metro: a pompous muddle of marble and porphyry, dreadful.

17 September
Had breakfast and packed our suitcases. At half-past eight, asked Intourist for a taxi to the station. Panic: no tickets or reservation had been arranged; our vouchers could only be used to pay for tickets, not as tickets. After extensive telephoning, took taxi to the station; everything sorted out at the last minute. We have been in the train since 10.11, en route to Siberia. Monotonous landscape, but the forests have wonderful autumn colours. We have a small two-person compartment with one easy chair and two beds, quite stuffy. The Chinese attendants are very friendly and helpful. Just had our [first] Chinese meal in the train: (1) strips of dried jellyfish in soya sauce with salted shrimp, (2) dark-green preserved eggs (with brown transparent gelatinous whites), (3) Sichuan-style goat's meat with peppered cabbage in soya sauce. My stomach is now feeling a little fragile.

Letter 1: Beijing, 24 September
Dear Puck,
We arrived safely in Peking yesterday evening after a long, tiring but extraordinarily interesting journey. I already wrote to you from

---

13   Sergey Tichvinsky (1918), Russian diplomat and academic. A China expert who was extremely active in Russian-Chinese academic relations.

Moscow and sent a card from Novosibirsk, but I just heard from Roland that Siberians sometimes steam the stamps off letters and throw the letter or postcard away. So it may be the case that you don't receive it – or Mam,[14] to whom I also sent a card from Novosibirsk. After Moscow, Siberia was an anti-climax: I have never seen such a dreary country, despite the beautiful autumn colours in the truly endless forests, and despite the wonderful landscape that you enter once you've passed Lake Baikal. Gloomy, poverty-stricken villages of tumbledown, bare wooden houses and huts; roads that are completely unpaved, which become pools of mud in the rainy season; and above all, poorly-clad and decidedly unfriendly people. Something happened that I would never have thought possible: at every station, groups of miserable paupers would come to the train to … beg! They were given food and cigarettes by the restaurant car, and a fat female Intourist official, who was also travelling in our carriage, clearly had the task of keeping them all quiet. She sent them scattering with a torrent of Russian and with cigarettes. A few times, they became threatening to our Chinese train and to the poor Chinese car attendant who had to stay at his post (legs visibly trembling) as long as the train was at a station. We saw tangible evidence of the Siberian paupers' anti-Chinese feeling: our train was pelted with stones (while moving) up to three times, and three window-panes were broken. These had to be repaired (evidently at Chinese request) by Russian workers before we left Siberia. One time, I saw one of the Chinese attendants walking round with a stone that had been chucked in, which must have weighed half a pound.

Aside from this, the journey went well: we had a comfortable compartment with our own washroom, reasonable meals, and nice conversations with some Chinese fellow travellers who were incredibly helpful.

---

14   Fenny Arendina Bulten-Kühlman (1898-1980), Erik's mother-in-law.

These fellow travellers were diplomats. Despite the high level of tension between China and the Soviet Union, they were still taking the Trans-Siberian express as usual:

19 September
In the evening, had a conversation in the corridor with two Chinese travelling with Gijs (Mr. Pei):[15] namely, Wang Guanghua (from Shanghai, married to a woman from Amoy, also speaks Russian) and the scholarly clerk Lei Teng. Talked about literature with the latter.

20 September
At Ilyanskaya this morning, had an early conversation with Gijs, who turns out to be the commercial counsellor at the Chinese embassy in Stockholm; he is called Pei Zesheng, lives in Peking, and comes from Shansi. A decent chap.

21 September
Naushki border station: endless checks on passports and currency. The Chinese helped us. Mr. Wang Guanghua took roubles from us and will pay us back with 45 yuan in Erlian[16] (otherwise we would never have seen the money again, thanks to bureaucracy: customs wanted to take it and give us a receipt that we would have to send to a bank in Moscow, which would send us a cheque in due time, and so on). Wang has been reassigned to Peking (from where?). Mr. Lei Teng comes from Warsaw, where he was the Chinese representative to the Chinese-Russian-Polish railway union; he has a month's leave, after which he will return (with our roubles).

15   A Chinese fellow traveller, whom they had clearly spotted earlier and who, for unknown reasons, had been given the nickname 'Gijs'.
16   The border station between China and Mongolia.

23 September
Long conversation with Gijs that helped us understand many things, including the continuity of family terminology and emotional ties (for example, vis-à-vis the older generation).

Mongolia was impressive for its unbelievably vast steppe, through which you travel for ten hours at a stretch. Saw nothing but undulating steppe; not a single tree. Sometimes a herd of horses or cattle, watched over by Mongolian horsemen in colourful costumes, once a herd of camels; and settlement after settlement of true Mongolian felt tents. Both upon entering and leaving Mongolia, we had a panic. Tek had been told by the Russian ambassador in The Hague that we would be able to get a Mongolian transit visa without any difficulty on the journey in, and that we would even be able to get one on the train – but that wasn't the case! The Mongolian customs official got shirty, said that the Russians were badly informed, and declared coolly that we would not be permitted to enter Mongolia without a proper visa. You'll understand that this made us nervous, as this was all happening at the border crossing at Sukhe Bator, a tiny settlement of five wooden houses in the endless steppe, and the next train to Peking coming only a week later! We were already starting to imagine ourselves pining away and dying of thirst, or freezing to death without any blankets. In the end, I brought in one of our Chinese fellow travellers, Wang Guanghua (a diplomat, we think), who can speak Russian. I explained everything in Chinese and he translated it into Russian. He really has the gift of the gab and pleaded our case; the fat tour guide (called 'Paulina') also came to help. In the distance we could hear the locomotive snorting impatiently, just a few minutes before departure. Mongol kept silently smiling. In the end, Paulina went off with him and came back just in time with a Mongolian paper for us to sign. A stamp in the passport and the train left. Still rattled, the four of us (including Mr. Wang) celebrated with a bottle of wine (ours) and a bottle of cognac (from Paulina's stash of gifts for bribes). Conversation was difficult: if Tek wanted to say something to fat Paulina, I had to translate it into Chinese, and Wang translated it into Russian, and Paulina's answer would come back in the same way via Wang and myself, to Tek. Good practice, in any case! When we left Mongolia, the trouble began all over again. We had a stamp but not a proper transit visa, said customs, and that wasn't enough. I just called Wang again, and he pleaded our case again (successfully), supported by Mr. Lei Teng, who could also speak some Russian.

Then we finally entered China! In Erlian we were met by an official from Luxingshe,[17] who offered us cigarettes and tea in the station's VIP room. We rose early the next morning so that we could see China. General impression: it is quite poor, of course, but infinitely better than Siberia. The harvest seems abundant and the people appeared to be dressed reasonably and well-fed. We saw many interesting things on the way, of course: villages and communes (but

17   The Chinese equivalent of Intourist, the state tourism agency.

also a remarkable number of small freestanding farms), the Great Wall, which we passed at Juyongguan, and imposing mountains.

At 8 p.m. we arrived in Peking (massive station), where we were met not only by the representative from Luxingshe, but also by Roland. We are now staying at the MINZU HOTEL (perhaps it's better to write MINZU FANDIAN for the Chinese postal service), CHANG'AN DAJIE, PEKING. Add ROOM NO. 545 to the address. It's a large modern hotel and we both have a double room with adjoining bathroom. That is where I'm writing this to you now.

The diary gives a better sense of how the arrival in Beijing, after eight days of travelling, must have been an exciting experience for the travellers:

23 September
As we left this area, evening fell and we approached Peking. Said a warm farewell to Wang and Lei (we helped Wang with his massive amount of luggage, including a complete Russian television set!) and looked on as he was met at Xizhimen Station by numerous family members (just like Lei). We went on, said goodbye to Pei in the train, and after a long, dark ride around Peking, reached the main station, which is incredibly large and modern and took just one year to build. At the station we were met not only by Mr. Zhao from Luxingshe (aged 30, speaks good French), but also, to our great surprise, by Roland. Went together to our hotel, which is new and modern and full of foreign guests (including many French, due to an industrial show, and also a large number of delegations for the national celebrations, including Africans with strange fur hats, Japanese, et cetera). Room no. 545 for me, 546 for Tek. Modern lifts with smiling girls, a post office with show-stamps, one dining room for Chinese cuisine and one for Western food.

I cannot yet say much about Peking; I have only a fleeting impression of great space and little traffic. As a first, quick visit, we took a short walk through the courtyards of the former imperial palace. It's incredibly large and impressive, but the restored parts in particular are too gaudy for me. Otherwise, everything is spick and span and, in the centre, very modern. The people in the street are immensely curious. They nudge each other and ask themselves what kind of people we are, and if they hear me say anything in Chinese, they look at me as though I must be from Mars. But everyone is unusually friendly and helpful, and the general feeling in the street is not in the least tense, as many people think. It's peaceful here, and you sometimes get the impression that people simply ignore the slogans that stare down at us everywhere (something you have to get used to, along with the 20-metre-high portraits of Mao Zedong).

Roland is making a huge effort for us. Yesterday he took us to his house straight after our arrival at the hotel, gave us something to eat and drink, made rooms available as necessary, picked us up again this morning to introduce us to Laboyrie (the *chargé d'affaires*),[18] will dine with us on Sunday, has arranged two Chinese tutors to teach me practical spoken language, and so on. He has a nice house, partly furnished in Chinese style, and a large garden with a lotus pond and a tennis court. Tek and I have been invited to dine with the *chargé d'affaires* this evening. Also spoke to the Luxingshe officials this morning: it seems that we will be able to get quite a lot done, and perhaps we will be able to spend the whole four months in China.

Other than that: we've unpacked our suitcases, rested a bit, and have enjoyed a few really good Chinese meals. We have to get used to everything; it all still feels very new and chaotic. I've put your

18   Until the 1970s the Netherlands only had a *chargé d'affaires*, not an ambassador, in the People's Republic of China. Although the Netherlands had recognized the People's Republic as early as 1950, relations between the two countries had soured shortly after the outbreak of the Korean War.

photos on the Chinese desk in my room, and sometimes when I look at them I feel homesick already – how will it be after a few months? Despite all the new and interesting things, I'm looking forward to coming home and to our shared adventure in Egypt.

Now dear Pucky, until the next letter or postcard; I will write lots to tell you everything that's going on.

Much love to you both, from Erik.

P.S. Tek sends his warmest greetings, and is also sitting writing (in Malay). My god, Tek can sleep! I don't know how he does it. Even during the panic in Mongolia, he fell asleep every now and then.

Erik at the Imperial Palace in Beijing.

Six weeks in Beijing

Letter 2: Beijing, 3 October

Dear Puck,

3 October, and no hotpot, eels or grapes.[19] I hope that the weather in Holland is as nice as it is here; after a few rainy days, we have wonderful autumn weather again. Roland gave me your letter on Sunday 27 September, he had received it on Saturday. This means that a letter (dated Sunday) takes a whole week to get here, if sent via the Consul-General in Hong Kong. I think that it won't take more than five days if sent directly. It's great to have your news! I have made a note of the reopening of the Ned. Hand. Mij. as the 'General Bank of the Netherlands'[20] for later in Hong Kong. I am writing everything down in my diary, including the most trivial things (such as the names of dishes I've eaten).

We are slowly starting to adjust to life in Peking. Our days are extremely busy, not only due to the events that Luxingshe is organizing for us, but also because we are wandering around all kinds of neighbourhoods, where we are learning and noting a great deal (and the big bosses at Luxingshe, who are not at all happy about this, are unable to do anything about it).

In the diary, we find out how this went:

24 September
Our first walk through the city, the two of us: went to the Xidan market and surroundings, strolled around everywhere

---

19   This is a reference to traditional Dutch celebrations to commemorate the Relief of the Siege of Leiden (1573-1574).
20   On 3 October 1964, the Nederlandsche Handelsmaatschappij and the Twentsche Bank merged to form the Algemene Bank Nederland, which would become ABN AMRO in 1990.

and looked at everything, went into shops, bought a cookie from an old lady in a small *hutong*,[21] et cetera. Interesting things everywhere, too many to write down. Toddlers in open-crotch pants, traditional Chinese pharmacies complete with (very expensive) Ginseng, weighed out in traditional scales; older women with bound feet, and to my great amazement, also a bare-breasted woman (suckling an infant), babies in bamboo carriages, et cetera, et cetera. Food abundant and very cheap by our standards. But we wondered how much one earns, for example, if one is selling tea on a stall, or one of the (sometimes very old) trishaw cyclists.[22]

Whatever the case, people usually look well fed; in the smaller *hutongs* there is a great deal of poverty, which is not surprising. People gape at us everywhere, of course, and stare and talk about us at length, particularly when it turns out that I speak some Chinese. In one small *hutong*, however, we were greeted formally by a whole pack of scouts (with raised hands)! An important lesson: it shows that the journalists' stories ('You're followed everywhere on foot by a guide and you can't make any contact with ordinary people') are utter nonsense. The explanation is obvious: journalists can't speak the language and are simply scared.

25 September
In the afternoon, wandered endlessly through the city. Had lunch in a gloomy snack bar, somewhere in the

21 A *hutong* is a traditional Chinese residential neighbourhood, in which people live in low houses around courtyards that are connected via narrow alleyways. At the beginning of the twentieth century, the majority of cities such as Beijing and Shanghai consisted of such neighbourhoods, but they have now become rare.
22 A three-wheeled cycle-taxi for two passengers, also known as a *betjak* in Indonesia.

Dongan Shichang: a meal of sweet biscuits and sweet *Lianzi tangzhou*. Tek also had sweet bean broth, and it all came to around Y. 1.40; very cheap, in other words. Naturally we were the talk of the town. Amusing phonetic mix-up: I ordered soup (*tāng*) and, thanks to my faulty pronunciation, was given *táng*, sickly-sweet doughnut balls, which I ate with reluctance. Wandered further (drank bike-pump beer 'à la pression' at a little stall). Tek bought a child's charm (!) and a bamboo fine-toothed comb for the museum from friendly shop manager. Ate *haitang* (star apple) on a stick with melted sugar; bought Peking-speciality candied fruits and ate them. Then we wandered through part of the palace gardens again and then along the western side of the palace city, through a poor neighbourhood to the south; visited Chengshan park (particularly struck by beautiful lotus pond and, in Tek's case, the large collection of demented goldfish in rows of pots). Finally had a delicious meal at a restaurant by the pond (lovely old rock and moss garden!). We ate rice with *hongshaoyu*, sea fish, pieces of meat with sweet pepper in soya, cabbage stalks in sauce, and pieces of roast chicken in soya; accompanied by an incredibly strong *baijiu* ('twice distilled'). Went home tired out (we'd been out from 12:30 until around 9 p.m., Tek since the morning).

Tek clearly took his immersion in everyday life even further than Erik:

2 October
Tek went to Tianqiao (it later proved that he (1) had a dreadful but extremely cheap cut and shave, (2) went to a wrestling match between sweaty wrestlers for the price of ten cents, and (3) ate lung and drank tea).

We've visited various great monuments, such as the Ming[23] tombs and accompanying reservoir, the Great Wall at Juyongguan, the tomb of Emperor Wanli, the summer palace, et cetera, I shall tell you more about it later; it is all very impressive. Unfortunately, there are also downsides. For one thing, all of the temples and many other historic buildings have been converted (inside) into schools, libraries and association buildings, so they can only be visited with the usual letter of introduction. The outside is nicely renovated and cared for, but on the inside the whole thing is often completely spoiled. Second (as Piet[24] in Bordeaux[25] said): only the most important monuments have been renovated, perhaps 2 or 3 per cent of the total; all the rest, such as the Peking city gates and numerous temples, and so on, are falling into sad disrepair and rotting away. And there is no alternative. China is desperately poor and full-scale renovation would cost billions. Yesterday, Roland and I visited a small, ancient lama temple in north-western Peking. The main building was closed; just one old lama lives there, who cares for the statues and dusts the altar, but he is isolated and did not appear. Families are living around the temple courtyards and in the outbuildings; children swarmed over the crumbling steps, washing hung on the pillars, and the tiled floor of the courtyards had been broken up everywhere to plant vegetables. The whole thing gave an impression of sad decline and indescribable poverty. And that is unfortunately the rule; the well-restored monuments that Luxingshe proudly shows off are actually great exceptions.

We watched the great procession on 1 October, of course, standing in a grandstand. It was indeed 'the biggest show on

---

23   The Ming dynasty ruled China between 1368 and 1644.
24   Piet van der Loon, sinologist and lecturer at Cambridge (later a professor in Oxford).
25   The conference in Bordeaux was the 'Junior Sinologues Conference', the precursor to the European Association of Chinese Studies.

earth'. In the square (the largest square in the world) there were more than 600,000 people; in the procession (rows of 60 people deep) there were more than 10,000, singing and marching, every conceivable type: metal workers, nurses, ethnic minorities such as Mongols and Tibetans in costume, numerous dance troops, the entire music conservatory and the whole concert-hall orchestra playing their instruments, also flower-waving Buddhist monks and Roman Catholic nuns, would you believe it, and so on. Wonderfully colourful, incredibly well-organized and with a terrifying degree of zeal that swept everyone along. For a Dutchman, it (luckily) remains mere show, but a show of truly impossible dimensions. The rest of the day, there was a kind of super-'3 October'[26] mood in the street: wonderful, the traffic blocked by masses of people wearing their Sunday best and eating and snacking, blaring radios everywhere, alternating with wildly tooting stuck cars, and in the evening the largest firework display one could imagine, in drizzling rain. The whole thing – at least, as far as the official events go – was a performance by a select group. It is impossible for us to comprehend. That a procession of 10,000 people could be composed solely of a select group is one thing, but that the 600,000-strong audience in Tiananmen Square could consist exclusively of selected delegations is beyond our comprehension. The whole square, as far as the eye could see, was full of neatly organized groups, every member of which was holding a colourful bouquet of artificial flowers or suchlike. The direction was perfect: on the signal, everyone lifted their bouquet in the air and shook it, and the whole square was instantly transformed into a sea of red flowers, with splendid yellow characters forming the figures '1949-1964' and the words 'Long Live Chairman Mao'. The rhythmic roaring of half a million voices, a 1,000-man orchestra playing the

26   Translator's note: another reference to the traditional Dutch celebrations marking the Relief of the Siege of Leiden.

music, and far in the distance, in the seat of honour, just a couple of millimetres high due to the distance, we saw a grey figure waving.

But those masses proved to be made up of individuals:

1 October
Two huge coincidences: first, from the grandstand we saw our travelling companions, Mr. Wang Guanghua and Lei Teng; energetic waving on both sides. And then we saw Roland and we took photographs of each other.

They also made the most of the national holiday in the afternoon:

In the afternoon, took a short taxi ride to Tianqiao. Hugely busy there with bustling market, including Mongolian wrestling and shadow theatre (which Zhao had not shown to Tek; he was evidently ashamed of such 'old-fashioned' entertainment).

In a small, dark and rickety theatre, we watched a series of scenes from a shadow play called *Hongyunya*.[27] Wonderful effects: *wugu*[28] grow from small to large, a sorceress transforms herself into all kinds of shapes; Zhu Bajie cries real tears! The manager of the establishment was evidently impressed by having foreign visitors and we did not have to pay. We must go back, and see if we can watch a performance from behind the scenes.

---

27 This is actually the title of a popular political animation film of 1962, 'Red Cloud Cliff'. The show appears to have been something very different, namely an episode of *Xiyou ji*, the well-known 'Journey to the West'.
28 Demons.

One could hardly imagine a greater contrast with the evening programme:

Yesterday evening, something similar: a kind of super singing-and-dancing performance on the stage of the People's Assembly Hall, with 3,000 participants on stage and an audience of 20,000. Again: selected 'delegations' and 'friends from abroad', huge and incredibly well organized. But it left a bitter aftertaste in my mouth. The music and dancing were technically perfect, but it was unbelievably kitsch. And ordinary people don't get a look-in.

But it was a chance to observe the party leaders:

During the meal, Liu Shaoqi held a speech.[29] Completely incomprehensible (Hunan dialect). At the end, we saw Chairman Mao when the guests of honour and VIPs went on stage. Massive applause, et cetera. An interesting evening, despite all the official nonsense.

We have met many ordinary people on our walks through the streets and alleyways of Peking. The upsides are: despite the poverty, everything is clean (even the narrowest alleyways are swept), and while people are dressed in worn clothing that's been patched a hundred times, they are no longer in rags. One seldom sees people who are evidently suffering from hunger; there is running water and electric lighting everywhere in Peking, and no beggars at all. Tips are resolutely refused, not just because of the fear of being 'reported', but also out of pride, even when no one is watching. And above all: the people are cheerful and friendly. The downsides are: drab poverty as soon as one leaves the impressive façade of the city centre (the

---

29   Second president of the People's Republic of China. Purged by Mao during the Cultural Revolution in 1967 and died of maltreatment in 1969.

only thing that most tourists ever see). There is clear overcrowding. It is said that the old houses built around small courtyards are home to 4-8 families, and it is very common for a father, mother and three children to share two small rooms. Wages range from 30 to 300 yuan a month (1 Y = 1.50 guilders),[30] and Y 300 is actually a top salary (for the most senior officials, including professors).

The influence of the regime is absolute and omnipresent. It extends right into working-class neighbourhoods, where traditional 'storytellers' tell their tales in the old style to a breathless audience – but no longer of ancient heroes, but of the battle between Chairman Mao and the dark forces of the Guomindang[31] and imperialism. Coincidentally, this afternoon we succeeded in getting to hear such a storyteller, who practised his craft with true virtuosity, using gestures, mime and musical accompaniment.

The diary describes it as follows:

3 October
Then Tianqiao: first tea in a working-class pub, drew looks, Tek managed to wheedle plastic finger-balls off an old man; then joined the audience of a modern *shuoshude* (telling a story about the underground Communist movement in Chongqing[32] during the war). A true virtuoso, wearing scholarly gown and with drum and castanets, beating a stone on the table, accompanied on the guitar, with the

---

30   In 1964 everything was still converted into Dutch guilders. When the euro was introduced, one guilder was worth 45 eurocents.
31   The Chinese Nationalist Party, founded in 1912, and the ruling party between 1928 and 1949 in the parts of China that were not under foreign occupation. After its defeat by the Communists in 1949, the Guomindang became established in Taiwan (Formosa), where it remained the only legal party until 1987.
32   During the Second World War, the capital of the Nationalist government of China.

periodic rattle in the spittoon. According to Tek, the style is completely traditional but the theme is new.

It has also been nice to be in contact with various Chinese of Indonesian origin, who live in Peking or are staying there during the holidays. We spoke with Wu Yixiu ('Go Ik-sioe',[33] a friend of Tek's brother-in-law and Wertheim,[34] and member of the Chinese People's Congress); Tek's childhood friend, Fu Dexi ('PaoTek-hi', an internist in Peking), with Tjan Tjoe-siem (Som's brother, from Jakarta, member of the Indonesian delegation to Peking) and above all with Lin Qingding (Li King-ting, a friend of Go Lam-san & Kitty). King-ting is especially kind; he is open and intelligent and gives (perhaps because of this) a tense and somewhat unhappy impression. Tek says that he used to be artistic, and in typical Tek fashion (by going on endlessly about jade and paintings, and by dragging him to art shops), tried to awaken the old flame in him. You could see King-ting becoming more confused by the minute. Finally, he said that he had renounced art, because 'if you live among the people, as we do, then there are so many more important things to do'. He didn't sound terribly convinced, though, and in the end he did buy a couple of paintings after all. For us it's important to hear these *huaqiao* living in China speak about their lives here. Sometimes they are critical, but on the whole they are genuinely enthusiastic (but they are all scientific types, of course, who consider certain things that we value highly to be relatively unimportant).

33 Southern Chinese pronunciation, also common in Indonesia.
34 Willem Frederik Wertheim, Marxist (later Maoist) sociologist and professor at the Municipal University of Amsterdam between 1946 and 1972. The opinions of Wertheim and Erik Zürcher would later diverge radically over the Cultural Revolution in China, which Wertheim embraced.

Roland is still doing his very best for us. Yesterday he visited various monuments with me again (in a large limo belonging to the CD),[35] and tomorrow he will spend the whole of Sunday with us, ending with a performance of Peking opera.

According to the diary, this was the second Peking opera in two days, for we read that on 3 October:

In the evening, had stew with rib of beef (Chinese-style) at Roland's, and then went to see Peking opera. *Yezhulin,*[36] very beautiful (same theatre as yesterday evening); the large audience included foreigners (mainly from embassies). According to Mieke, hardly anyone used to go to Peking opera, but now that it is about to disappear (or rather, now that it's not really permitted any more), everyone is suddenly going. The French ambassador, who shook my hand limply, was sitting behind us. In the interval an Indian diplomat went so far as to declare categorically that these performances of classical opera were only being put on for foreigners around the 1 October celebrations. We shall see.

Three pieces, the first of which we missed because we were late (something from *Shuihu*).[37] The other two: *Jiangxiang he* (reconciliation between general and minister, with old-patriotic leanings) and the well-known *Sancha kou*

35 *Chargé d'affaires.*

36 'The forest of the wild boar', an adaptation of an episode from the sixteenth-century novel *Shuihuzhuan*. This play could be put on because, according to the prevailing interpretation at that time, it showed how in ancient times even the most loyal subjects were forced to rebel due to the greed and unfairness of the rulers.

37 *Shuihu*, or *Shuihu zhuan*, 'The water banks'. Sixteenth-century novel about noble bandits. Known in the West in the translation by Pearl Buck as 'All Men Are Brothers'.

(mock battle in 'darkness') episodes from the popular tale *Yangjia jiang* ('The generals of the Yang family'). Wonderful costumes, music brief and monotone. Sign language et cetera perfect, of course.

Classical Peking opera clearly went down better than modern hybrids:

26 September
In the evening, went with Mr. Ni to a musical performance by members of the Chinese conservatory, in a theatre not far from Chang'an Dajie. Social-realist leanings; in itself, an interesting experiment to use traditional Chinese instruments in a Western orchestral way, but unfortunately very kitsch. The last number was a great lyrical drama about the history of Changyu Shancun; very stereotyped and dripping with tasteless pathos. It would be better to use traditional forms and timbre. By contrast, a very good solo on the *pipa*,[38] and a good solo by straight and transverse flutes. We have been told that Mr. Ni is 'better qualified' as a guide, but very little of his quality shines through, to put it mildly. In any case, history and music are not his strongest points, and his English is much worse than Mr. Zhao's French. We suspect that he was assigned to us because the better guides were needed for the delegations at the national celebrations, but perhaps we're underestimating his knowledge. We drowned the kitsch after-taste with two glasses of exceptionally strong Chinese brandy, known as *Maotai* (bottle cost Y. 3.40).

---

38   Chinese lute.

Roland's large garden (it belongs to the legation, complete with swimming pool and tennis court!) was transformed into a desert of bits of wood, metal and cardboard. For there was a south-westerly wind on 1 October, meaning that all the burnt-out containers and remains of the super-fireworks came down in their neighbourhood – sometimes burnt-out spherical containers of 30 cm in diameter! The Chinese staff were delighted. For the projectiles included silk parachutes (for the torches that are meant to descend slowly), which they will make into shirts and underwear.

In the meantime, I have had lessons from my two Chinese tutors, both fringe figures who used to be immensely rich. They have now fallen out of favour and scrape together a living by teaching. They are old-school scholars, highly erudite and civilized, and I really enjoy their lessons.

This is the first mention of the gentlemen Wu and Xu, to whom the diary frequently refers. They were an important source of information for Erik:

24 September
My future tutors, Wu and Xu (Wu is Manchu, his father was chief of the Manchu bodyguard, a stately old gentleman).

27 September
Went to Roland's for 7 p.m.; we went with him and Wu and Xu to have an absolutely delicious meal at a celebrated Shaguoju *fandian* dating from late Ming (!), cooked in 400-year-old pots; every cut of pork: brains, stomach, temples, soup, intestines, et cetera, in *chambre séparée*. Wu tells me that the notorious monkey brains of Hong Kong and Canton are no legend, and that he was never able to eat them. Wu and Xu are both 'old school' scholars, very learned and civilized. Moreover, Wu speaks exceptionally clear and

comprehensible Peking Chinese. He has an inexhaustible knowledge of Peking (history of local customs), on which Tek draws eagerly.

29 September

Spent the first two hours of this morning with Mr. Wu, 'Hanson C. Wu, Instructor of the Chinese Language', see card); translated (orally) a text from English Peking book, first in *baihua*,[39] then in *wenyan*;[40] then chatted about history, and so on; it went well. Phoned Roland beforehand about payment: I should pay after one month (Y. 30?). Among other things, Mr. Wu told me about the old Jesuit graves in Peking: the eighteenth-century (and perhaps also a few seventeenth-century) ones were moved to the area of the airfield (they used to be where the station is now). But the oldest and most interesting ones (Ricci,[41] Schall,[42] De Ursis,[43] et cetera) are by the old Beitang,[44] now a school, so it's probably not possible to visit them. He also told me that the remains of the Mongol wall north of Peking are still there, not far.

---

39 Vernacular Chinese.

40 Classical Chinese.

41 Matteo Ricci (1552-1610), the founder of the Jesuit mission in China.

42 Johann Adam Schall von Bell (1592-1666), Jesuit and missionary in Beijing from 1630. He was thrown into prison in 1664 for high treason and for spreading a malignant religion. The original death sentence was revoked after the occurrence of an earthquake and other striking natural phenomena. Father Schall died of natural causes a year later.

43 Sabatino de Ursis (1575-1630), Italian Jesuit, missionary in China from 1603 and exiled to Macao in 1620, where he died. De Ursis could thus not have been buried in Beijing.

44 The Jesuit-built library of the northern church, one of the old Catholic churches in Beijing. It contained thousands of European works (primarily gifts from the Pope and Italian renaissance princes), opening up European science of the sixteenth and seventeenth centuries to China.

We are still waiting for definitive notice of the duration of our stay. In any case, we will be able to stay two months (according to the stamps in our passports), but further plans are still under consideration. It is very probable that we will be able to stay in China until January. The Luxingshe official (our guide Mr. Ni, who is very stupid and incompetent, a real old wretch) has said that he can help me get hold of a winter coat, without the need for a ration card.

We have been to the 'antiques' market a couple of times. Very nice things and not expensive, but all the good pieces are gone. This afternoon we went to a jade market; a huge amount of jade, sometimes of exceptional quality, but like anywhere else in the world, the best quality is not cheap, and really first-class translucent green jade is priced at around the same level as emerald. Aided by Tek, I'm in the process of negotiating over a pair of earrings and a few smaller things. Tek is having fun and buying things to his heart's content, both for the museum and for himself. He buys the craziest things, such as cricket cages, little jade boxes for toothpicks, an amber thumb-ring, amulets made of punched tin, an ivory fine-toothed comb, and so on, and so on. Both the sellers and our guide clearly think that he's mad. This afternoon he started a conversation with a very grubby old man who was sitting playing with two little homemade plastic balls, and he talked and laughed for as long as it took to be given the balls as a present.

Dear Puck, I can keep going like this, because every day brings something new. Will you write soon to let me know how things are going? Here, time is flying, but I'm afraid that in Oegstgeest the rainy autumn days will be dragging by. It will be wonderful to see each other again after such a long separation – your portraits are a poor replacement! Would you say hello to the neighbours for me? I've sent them a postcard.

Goodbye my darlings, all my love from Eerft/Pap

Gan Tjiang Tek.

Letter 3: Beijing, 10 October

Dear Puck,

Due to the strange 'timeless' life that we're leading here, I have lost track of the days, and I don't exactly know when I last wrote (clearly I forgot to note it down in my diary).[45] But I believe that it must already be more than a week ago, around 3 October, so I will bring you both quickly up to date again with our adventures.

Again: so many impressions in the past week that I don't know where to begin.

He could have begun here, for example:

4 October
Visited various temples with Roland in the morning. The Dazhongshi, with its gigantic clock (the largest in the world), completely covered in Sutra text, Yongzheng

---

45   This isn't actually true; Erik made a careful note of every letter in his diary.

era (five monks live here, *Chan*,[46] with their own large vegetable garden, which looks pretty good). Afterwards went to a lovely lama temple just outside the city (with its carved white marble pagoda, the tops of which were destroyed by the Japanese and are now restored). Shown around by the 77-year-old lama who has been living at the temple for 36 years (there is some kind of sanatorium in the temple).

In the afternoon, went with Roland and Mieke to Xishan, the hunting park of Qianlong with its famous glazed pagoda. The park (on a mountainside) is called Xiangshan ('fragrant hills'); beautiful location and many interesting monuments (including the 'spectacles lake' and a well-kept nunnery, in a courtyard with a beautiful pond; a few Chinese visitors, including a man who was lovingly pulling the claws off a live mantis). Had a picnic there, after a vertiginous climb up a narrow, steep path.

Having descended, returned to Peking. On the way, saw a village (site of old Catholic church and graveyard; everything had been destroyed and broken). In a field there was an ugly *Putai*[47] (with a fat stomach) from the Chenghua period, with two accompanying steles and, remarkably enough, a whole row of recently dug graves, including some that had evidently been dug up and moved.

Erik selected a very different subject with which to start the letter, however:

First of all: our correspondence. On 4 October Roland gave me your letter dated 24 September (i.e. it took nine days to come), on 6 Octo-

---

46   The Chinese branch (and origin) of Zen Buddhism.
47   Image of Maitreya, the buddha of the future.

ber your letter dated 1 October (sent directly: it took just five days), and today, 10 October, Erik-Jan's letter from the 3rd (although the stamp shows that it was posted on the 5th, i.e., it took five days to get here). We should thus allow for five days if letters are sent directly.

I have sent the neighbours another card, as a small token of thanks for their kindness to you. Tek has been down in recent days, mainly because he hasn't received a single letter from his family since he arrived. 'Oh well', he says gloomily, 'I'm used to it, they're all married and they don't know what it's like to be lonely.' Ah, poor thing! Evidently a further reason for his depressed mood is the dismissive attitude of the Chinese government (represented by member of congress Wu Yixin, on whom we have called a number of times) with regard to accepting Chinese emigrants from Indonesia. Tek's brother (a geologist) seems to be having a particularly difficult time there and wants to come to China. But the issue is not being taken seriously here; on the contrary. I'm able to understand the Chinese officials' attitude a bit, now that I've got to know various *huaqiao* here better, and above all Li King-ting (the husband of the well-known Mary from Fuzhou). He's a kind, warm fellow, sensitive, and despite having obediently memorized his lessons, is decidedly unsuited to this life in China, with 14 hours of hard work a day and no form of amusement or luxury. He clearly enjoys talking to us, as we come from the West and do not speak about the usual topics or in slogans. Many like him are insufficiently 'adjusted'. Roland told me that the embassy even gets letters almost every week (clandestine, of course) from *huaqiao* who want to come to Holland because they feel so miserable in China.

The diary also contains entries on the contact with the 'overseas Chinese'.

5 October
In the evening we had a very tasty 'East Indian' meal at the house of the Wu Yixiu family (accompanied by Pao Tek-hi and his ugly wife Hiang). We spent a long time admiring his wonderful collection of jade and snuff bottles; excellent taste and good pieces, also household effects. The interior was full to overflowing. They used to be extremely rich (they were allowed to keep their fortune and sold part of the collection to a museum, too).

11 October
Tek and I visited the house of Pao Tek-hi (with his wife Hiang). Li King-ting was also there. We drank coffee, lunched on East Indian food, and then all went to Taoranting park, south of Niujie. Walked, ate chestnuts, watched the little boats on the pond, et cetera. A lazy day (although with a lot of walking); we talked a lot, including about the past and future of China, with King-ting, who is keen to hear our impressions. 'One becomes so one-sided here over time.' Really?!? Tek-hi's house and interior are frightfully bare and shabby. Only idealism and the irrevocability of one's choice could keep one going in such circumstances.

I now know everything there is to know about jade (helped by Tek and my two Chinese tutors, the old scholars Wu and Zu). Three characteristics: (1) colour, (2) lustre and (3) translucency. Ideal colour: green as grass; best lustre: like a drop of water or, even better, like a drop of oil; and finally, half-translucent, like emerald. Jade of that quality is only to be found here at the Palace Museum. I took a photo of a small screen there, 20 cm by 45 cm, ± 1 cm thick – worth a fortune of a few million, if one reckons that jade like that costs around 3-4,000 yuan per cm^3. I'm doing my best to get something nice for you. There are also other kinds of jade: the whitish sort that the Chinese value very highly, from which you can buy beautiful bracelets, carved animals and suchlike for a reasonable price.

Tek is helping me to choose from the better, older pieces; I think that I will buy just a few of these things, ideal as souvenirs to give or to keep. A great many of them are on sale here, but many are extremely kitsch or trashy-gimmicky, which I'm not keen on. Tek also helped me to pick out a few pieces of porcelain: two lovely little *sang-de-boeuf* vases (not old, but they have a wonderful colour and glaze), and perhaps I'll also get a piece in apple green. I'm also thinking about an old Chinese bow in a case. Tek is buying truly crazy quantities of art and objects for the museum, ranging from cricket cages and jade toothpick-pots to wooden children's potties, to the despair of our guide and the great amusement of the Chinese public.

Luckily our Chinese is improving, so the guide is generally superfluous. We often go into the city without him, which is so peaceful.

But Erik also made serious purchases (see also the illustration on page 54):

9 October
A day of perusing and buying. Slept in. At 10 a.m. we took the car (without Ni) to Liulichang,[48] where I bought a seal and had it carved (Y. 14) by the famous seal-carver, Wei Changqing.[49] Tek bought various seals. Then on to the cal-

48 Neighbourhood in Beijing traditionally known as a centre for the trade in antiques, arts and crafts. During Erik and Tek's visit it still consisted of traditional stone houses, but it has since been 'done up' as a tourist site.
49 Wei Changqing (? -1978), founder of the Cui Wen Ge art centre in Beijing and an important seal-carver. Worked with Xu Huanrong on the inscriptions for Mao

The scroll. With thanks to Robert Price (National Museum of Ethnology, Leiden).

ligraphy shop, where I bought a horizontal scroll by Liang Qichao[50] (Y. 8) and a vertical scroll by Kang Youwei[51] (Y. 10). Took the latter to Rongbaozhai[52] to have it re-mounted (Y. 14). Tek also bought scrolls by Kang and Liang, plus a few other things.

These met the approval of a real Chinese scholar:

10 October

Had a class with Xu in the morning. Read *Shuihu*[53] (went well). Xu thinks very highly of my scroll by Liang Qichao.

Zedong and Zhou Enlai on the Monument to the People's Heroes on Tiananmen Square.

50   Liang Qichao (1873-1929), one of the most important pro-Western reformers and intellectuals in China around 1900. Also worked as a journalist and translator.

51   Kang Youwei (1858-1927). Well-known reformer from the late Manchu Empire, and also a famous calligrapher. Liang's tutor.

52   Rongbaozhai: a firm that has specialized in block printing and calligraphy since the end of the 19th century.

53   One of the four great novels of classical Chinese literature.

I think that it's a good idea for you to go to Seefeld, although I do wonder whether a more southern and sunnier place wouldn't be nicer. When the sun shines in the mountains it's fantastic, but can you be sure that the sun will shine? In any case, it will be better than spending the so-called 'holidays' in Holland. And once Christmas and New Year are over, we can start counting the days – then we'll see each other in just nine or so weeks! I often feel a mounting sense of homesickness, especially now that the excitement of the first introduction to China is over and wandering through Peking is starting to become routine. Sometimes I long to hear a familiar sound – even Radio Veronica![54] Everything is different and unfamiliar here. I heard Tek sigh today, 'I don't give a damn, you know – I wish I were happily at home with my motorbike and my cacti!' By the way, did you know that he's seriously planning to sink all his money in a Lancia when he gets back? He can get a really good one, second-hand, for only 20,000 guilders.

The food (which you asked about, didn't you?) is beyond all praise. The food at the hotel is good, but the city has specialized restaurants that make the best restaurant in Holland look like a greasy soup kitchen. Some time ago, with Roland and our tutors Wu and Xu, we ate at the famous Shaguoju restaurant, which dates from the late Ming period (± 1600). The food is cooked in 350-year-old earthenware pots on a huge stove that is just as old. All of the dishes consist of pork and are prepared in the most refined way. Every part of the pig is used: among other things, we ate dishes containing pigs' brains, ears, stomachs, temples (!), tongue, trotters and large intestines. Sometimes a sauce contains as many as twenty herbs. After the meal we visited the kitchen. Even in the finest restaurant one eats at a bare table covered in grease spots, and the interior is bare and utterly cheerless. But the food makes up for it all.

54   At that time, commercial broadcasting was still banned in Holland.

It's great that you went to the party at Hans',[55] graced with Frits[56] on the piano. I'm familiar with the new study programme; a while ago, I put much of it together with Dirk[57] and Hans. Hopefully Van Gulik's[58] appointment in Tokyo will go through, that would work out well for us. He has thus clearly <u>not</u> been appointed in Utrecht, perhaps due to obstruction from Leiden? I could ask Roland, but as you know, he gives little away. For the rest he's extremely helpful and kind, just like the *Chargé d'Affaires*, Laboyrie. Tek and I will soon go to Laboyrie's for dinner 'en famille'; I believe that Tek has stolen Mrs. Laboyrie's heart by tactically praising her worthless collection of porcelain.

I could write hundreds of pages on China, of course. But as time goes on, my general impression of the country is actually the same as in the first week. It's a very positive impression: the country is still desperately poor, and is being built up by combined forces with incredible zeal. There's no repressive police regime (indeed, you see very few policemen in the street). The people are cheerful and relaxed, and they treat each other and also us as foreigners in a friendly and warm way. This is something you find everywhere, even in the narrowest alleyways and taverns. I would dare to say that we have had more intense contact with Peking than any other Dutch visitors. First, we can make ourselves understood; second, we wander around everywhere, eating cookies at stalls surrounded by the barrow-men and char-ladies; and third, we frequently speak with the people who work here and who have lived in Peking for years.

There is no war-like atmosphere. And (as Roland remarked) everyone's attention is so focused on solving the massive domestic

55   Hans Blijerveld, student assistant and later librarian at the Institute of Sinology in Leiden.
56   Frits Vos, Professor of Japanese in Leiden.
57   Dirk Jonker, member of the academic staff at the Institute of Sinology.
58   Robert van Gulik, sinologist, Dutch diplomat and author of the celebrated *Judge Dee* detective novels.

construction and production problems that it would be absurd to imagine that the Chinese were also dreaming of unleashing a huge war. We would find such a severe regime intolerable. But if one looks around here, one increasingly realizes that it is the only real remedy for an underdeveloped region.

I have spoken with 'officials' a few times (something I have to do in the framework of our show-project for the ZWO).[59] I'm always given a polite reception, but you learn little from such discussions; just the well-known slogans and stereotypical positions that one finds in every book and every party brochure. Instead we have to make the most of our informal contacts, and mainly from our walks. It's a tiring existence; we're shattered every evening. But my health is OK, I'm getting enough sleep and enough to eat, so you mustn't worry!

It's gradually getting cooler here; I'm wearing long johns and will soon buy a sheep's wool lining for my raincoat. Thick fur coats are not expensive here (from Mongolia: ± 200 guilders for a very warm one); but what could I do with such a thing?

Dear Pucky, I will stop here, because I could quite easily carry on for 50 pages. All the details are all in my diary, which I write every evening – to the increasing discomfort of Tek, who has yet to write one page of his diary and has yet to take a single photo.[60] (He forgot to bring the instruction manual for his complicated camera!!)

That's all until the next letter. I'll look out for a message from you, and I'll write again soon.

Goodbye dearest, a hundred kisses from Eerft.

---

59 According to the diary, the project was about strengthening academic ties with China and establishing an exchange programme.
60 Tek did in fact take photos during the journey. The collection of his photos is kept at the National Museum of Ethnology in Leiden (information from Oliver Moore).

PS: we have moved to new rooms at the front of the hotel, for the sun. I'm now in room no. 518. It's not important – I'll get your letters in any case! Bye. Eerft.

Letter 4: Beijing, 18 October

Dear Puck,

The post appears to be in a great muddle. The day before yesterday (Friday) I got your letter dated 11 October, in which you wrote, among other things, that I should ignore your previous letter, which you had written in desperation because you hadn't heard anything from me. And this morning, two days later, I received the first letter, dated 7 October! In any case, I'll write a long letter every Sunday; this seems to me to be the best way to continue from now. But we can clearly say nothing with certainty about when the letters will arrive in Holland, although it normally seems to take 5-6 days. I send postcards, etc., sporadically. For example, I should still send a card to the Heestermans,[61] also on account of the Raghavendra Char case.[62] So I'm sorry that you sometimes have to wait, but it's really the fault of the postal service.

This was a week of important events, both for us and the wider world.

In relation to us: last Friday (the 16th) we were given official notice that we would not be permitted to stay in China for longer than two months, and that we would eventually cross the border at Canton on 23 November. This is disappointing, of course, not least because it means that the trip to the far interior (Luoyang and Xi'an)[63] will not go ahead (Luxingshe: 'We don't have an office there'; which is absurd). Still, there's nothing we can do about it.

---

61 Jan Heesterman (1925-2014) had just been appointed Professor of South Asian history in Leiden in 1964, a position that he would hold until 1990.
62 Indian student in Leiden, later librarian at Durham University in England.
63 Popular tourist destinations today.

We will therefore spend only thirteen more days in Peking, just enough for one more exchange of letters. I will keep writing during the journey, of course, but you won't be able to send me any letters during those weeks. Should you need to get in touch in an emergency, write to our *Chargé d'Affairs* in Peking. He will be able to find out where I am at any given time and possibly phone me there or send a telegram. In Hong Kong I will immediately let you know where we are staying, for example by sending a direct telegram. There is still a faint chance that Luxingshe will go back on its decision. I've raised the matter with Laboyrie (the *Chargé d'Affairs*), and he is going to protest on behalf of the Dutch government and emphatically request the revocation of our 'sentence'.

It is not entirely clear why Luxingshe is being so difficult. Laboyrie said that they find us 'scary': we can speak the language, we don't stick to the beaten tourist track and we wander through the city's shady neighbourhoods. Our interests are strange (me with my love of Buddhist things, Tek buying everyday objects) and we ask all kinds of difficult questions (for example, about public servants' salaries). That's Laboyrie's opinion. Tek thinks that there is also a wider political background, particularly the Chinese atomic bomb, which is naturally the talk of the town here (as well as Nikita's leaving office).[64] Nikita's disappearance from the scene might lead to fraternization between China and Russia. The Chinese atomic bomb is likely to lead to many extra votes for Goldwater[65] and, as a result, also thwart the Russian-American rapprochement. If that is the case, then it's all over for the Chinese rapprochement with Western Europe and China's need to establish scientific contact with Western

64   Nikita Khrushchev (1894-1971). Took over from Stalin in 1953 as leader of the Communist Party of the Soviet Union and held this position until he was deposed in 1964. The break with China took place under his leadership, but he was also the one to provide China with the technology for the atomic bomb.
65   Senator Barry Goldwater (Arizona). The Republican challenger to President Lyndon Johnson in the elections of 1964; he was soundly beaten.

Europe. My visit has thus become less valuable to the Chinese, hence our two-month stay. Very clever reasoning on Tek's part, but maybe too far-fetched.

Whatever the case, we will most likely be in Hong Kong in around five weeks' time, and we will have to hold out there for around two months. There is enough to do in Hong Kong and perhaps we will be able to visit another island in the neighbourhood, so we will get through somehow.

We've had a very busy week, as usual, packed with more or less official visits, excursions, walks and shopping. Two of the visits were interesting and useful. On Tuesday (13 October) we were invited to the house of one of the most senior leaders, Guo Moruo, the former minister of education and now President of the Academy of Sciences, among other things.[66] He lives in a splendid house with a large garden. We stayed around 45 minutes, as usual drinking luke-warm tea and conversing formally. On this occasion we were not accompanied by Mr. Ni, our hopeless interpreter, but by the director of Luxingshe, Mr. Gu. From time to time, Guo Moruo, being the more senior of the two, indicated with an elegant gesture of his finger that we should see this or that, orders that were duly noted down by Gu. Among other things, we should be able to visit Zhoukoudian (where the Peking Man was found some time ago); very few Westerners have managed to get that far.

Even more interesting was the visit to Xia Nai, the celebrated archaeologist and director of the Archaeological Institute in Peking. We talked for a long time and he showed us the institute's collection. Unfortunately, private conversation with such figures is impossible. One is always received in the official reception room, with its 'suite' and tea-table, the guests on the sofa and the host plus one or

66 Guo Moruo (1892-1978) was a scholar and archaeologist/historian who had done part of his training in Japan. He had been a member of the Communist Party since 1927.

more official/interpreters/watchers in the armchairs, and endlessly-refilled cups of tea on the table. Questions are formulated and answered, then a visit to the institute (or office, or lab, or museum, et cetera), guided by the director, and finally the signing of the guest book, when one is asked to write some gushing endorsement or another. That's been the pattern many times.

We have managed to have many personal conversations with Tek's *Huaqiao* friends in China. But they are not firm ground on which to build, either: they are medics (for the most part), with that well-known, limited range that is typical of medics, and they are naturally somewhat naïve, with a patriotism that has been nurtured by extremely one-sided information. King-ting is the most intelligent and is thus also prey to hesitation, especially after the rather sharp political debates he has with Tek, who came down on him mercilessly. Not so much for the sake of politics, but more because he was in a foul mood (for he'd heard the news about the two-month stay permit the afternoon before, and felt the need to take his ill-feeling out on someone).

Tek evidently went far, certainly by Chinese standards:

13 October
Heated discussion about politics and other issues, initiated by a torrent of obscenities from Tek, while his incredulous audience listened. They are well-behaved, pious boys, and the two sides are utterly unable to comprehend each other.

But sometimes they got on really well:

16 October
We had a visit from Li King-ting in the evening. Cross-dressing in Tek's room with theatrical costumes and chatted

companionably until around midnight. After that time there's no taxi to be had in Peking, so Ting left.

Tek is still buying things. His room has become a kind of bizarre warehouse. Among other things, he's bought two complete costumes for Peking opera (which indeed appears to be dying out rapidly), huge things full of gold thread, embroidery and satin, with wonderful crowns, beards and buskins. There is still a lot available here, although it is not very old stuff. Sometimes the things cannot be dated but are definitely old. I've bought a few nice things, some worth much more than others, but all high-quality pieces (also in Tek's opinion): some porcelain (oxblood, transformation red, apple green); some jade, a few scrolls, an antique inkstone and an old wooden brush tray, et cetera. I'll send the heavier things with Tek's stuff for the museum and I will seek them out on my return. There's no more room in my suitcase.

We've visited the *Chargé d'Affaires* a couple of times, Laboyrie and his wife; a nice couple, although rather unintelligent people, of course, of the well-known diplomatic type: talkative without saying very much, always cheerful, et cetera. We ate with them 'en famille' and went shopping with them. Tek offered his assistance, but they have an irresistible urge to pick out the very worst pieces. But they are very friendly and helpful with everything and certainly not reactionary in a political sense.

Next Tuesday we're having dinner with the whole staff of the Peking mission at the secretaries' (held every year). Next Friday there's a large dinner at Laboyrie's, which will include Huan Xiang, the junior minister of Foreign Affairs, Xie Li (the former Chinese *Chargé d'Affaires* in Holland) and Mr. Wei of the Foreign Cultural Relations Office. It will be the perfect occasion to state coolly and clearly that it's a poor show to allow me only two months here, for goodness' sake.

According to the diary, Erik also expressed his displeasure clearly to the guide, Ni, undoubtedly in the belief that it would be passed on:

19 October
I've told Ni that I've had to conclude from the restrictions on our stay-period that the Chinese government attaches no importance to the establishment of contact, and that I shall therefore cancel all remaining official visits. Furthermore, that I've brought certain matters to the attention of the Dutch authorities, including in relation to China's desire to send twelve Chinese students to Holland. I hope that Luxingshe will accept the consequences. 'Love cannot be one-sided.' Enough.

Roland's still being very helpful. Today I went with Roland, Mieke and the children to the Ming tombs outside Peking, had a picnic, and later ate at their place. Back at the hotel at 11 p.m. (where I'm writing this now). Our party also included a certain Mr. Hendriksen: a horticultural seed breeder (strange profession!) who had spent three weeks in Inner and Outer Mongolia and had many very interesting things to say. Dinner at Roland's is a crazy experience. In the heart of Peking: first, Dutch-style drinks with savoury snacks from Verkade,[67] then potatoes in gravy with vegetables, preceded by soup as a starter and followed by dessert (chocolate pudding), accompanied by an Amstel beer, and then Dutch coffee and spiced biscuits. All served up by silent Chinese. Did I tell you that on 3 October we ate hotpot with rib of beef *à la Chinoise* at Roland's?

The weather has cheered up again: it's clear and sunny, but there's starting to be a chill in the air and in the evenings it's already

---

67 Translator's note: Verkade is a Dutch food manufacturing company famous for its biscuits and chocolate.

quite cold. I'm getting by with jumpers and long johns. I won't buy a coat or anything like that for those two weeks in the north. The sun will shine in Hong Kong, perhaps more than we'd like! Hendriksen told me worrying stories about the prices of hotels et cetera in Hong Kong and Japan. But he's an important businessman and the hotels will have been aware of that (40-50 guilders per person).

Dear Pucky, the pages are full and I also believe that I've told you the most important things.

At this time, however, the diary also describes things that are not necessarily important, but are still interesting, such as this insight into the Chinese power supply in 1964:

12 October

Light rain. Luckily Ni hadn't made any appointments. We went to the Forbidden City in the morning. Wandered around and looked at the huge collection of bronzes. There is so much to see that it's impossible to look carefully, you're constantly distracted. Famous pieces, too much crammed in, but with good popular explanations in the side-rooms of the palace. The electricity here is evidently strictly rationed; the exhibition galleries are only half-lit. After eating, we'll buy a pocket torch and will use it to look at the rest of the collection. A great day.

[In the end] we didn't go to the collection. The weather is too dark and it's impossible to find a torch in the city.

19 October

In the morning I went on my own to the Forbidden City. I spent a long time looking at the staggeringly rich Song[68]-

68   The Song dynasty ruled most of China between 970 and 1127, and ruled the southern half of the country for an additional one-and-a-half centuries.

Qing[69] department. Paid particular attention to painting and calligraphy. Many celebrated pieces; it proved much later that these very famous pieces were only brought to Peking to be exhibited on the occasion of the national holiday, so I was lucky. Unfortunately, no electric light; bring a torch on the next visit. Display good, not too packed. Buddhism completely neglected in explanations (everything is simply 'Foxiang' – 'Statue of Buddha'). In the left wing (Yuan[70]-Qing section), large photos of works that have been taken to Taiwan, with suitable captions. Also the Yuan fresco, which has been re-built (it had been sawn into sixty pieces by a Peking trader).

21 October
With Ni's help, we got hold of a torch; thus armed, we went to the Forbidden City for paintings et cetera. Looked at a large number of things from Liuchao[71] to early Song, mainly paintings and porcelain.

Keep your spirits up when you're bored (that's easy to say, I know), and don't worry if my letters sometimes take a while to come. The postal service clearly isn't working well, but I do write regularly! Lots of love to the two of you, and until the next letter. Bye bye!
Kisses, Eerft

Letter 5: Beijing, 23 October
Dear Puck –
I'm writing again, even though it isn't Sunday yet (it's the 23rd; that's to say, we've been in Peking for a whole month). You never know

69   Qing was the dynastic name of the Jurchen/Manchu emperors, the last dynasty of the Chinese empire. They ruled from 1644 to 1912.
70   The Mongol Yuan dynasty ruled between 1260 and 1368.
71   'The six dynasties', 4th-6th century AD.

where you are with these Chinese and their impenetrable ways. No sooner had I told you that we wouldn't be allowed to stay more than two months, there was a new development. This was in part thanks to the matter of the student exchanges, and partly, too, to help from Roland and Laboyrie. Shortly after my arrival, I'd had a lengthy discussion about student exchanges with the head of the Europe section of the Organization for International Cultural Relations. The people there were evidently aware of the importance of the issue, that is to say, of the importance of staying on friendly terms with me, to some extent. For another thing, Roland contacted the Chinese authorities directly and made it clear that if I were to have only two months here, I would have little time and few opportunities to promote Chinese educational interests! At any rate, yesterday Tek and I had lunch with some bigwigs from Luxingshe and the Organization for International Cultural Relations, and after much careful skirting around the issue and rubbish about the weather and so on, we were made to understand that we would actually be able to go to Xi'an and Luoyang, and that we would also be able to complete the rest of our programme. We weren't told exactly how long we'd have, but I think we'll be able to count on three months, if not more. The Organization for International Cultural Relations will assist us during our travels in those places where Luxingshe has no representation. All in all, then, a new and positive development. But it does mean that we have to draw up new travel plans again, and so on. And we are not yet sure when exactly we are to leave Peking. My suggestion would be that if you'd like to write to me again before I leave Peking (which according to the last report would be 31 October, but this is up in the air again), please do go ahead and do so. That's because I'm assuming that Luxingshe will get the letters and (having read them, or not) will forward them on to me, wherever I am. Hey ho. So, things are looking up again! The constant uncertainty has been making us touchy; we'd been at the point of saying, 'That's it, enough, we're off. We'll leave for Hong Kong tomorrow.' But to be honest, we'd only be harming ourselves if we were to do that. So we'll just have to keep going and make the best of it.

Tek's not having an easy time, either; he has to register, label, pack and send off the objects he's bought, more than 200 of them, and it's taking him days of work. The uncertainty of our departure date means that he's been living on the edge of a volcano: will he manage to get everything sent off in time? How will he get the money transferred from the museum, when and to where? Nerves have set off his stomatitis again, and he currently speaks as though he's got three hot potatoes in his mouth. This evening we're having dinner at Laboyrie's, by the way, so I'll wear my best suit. I can put everything in the wash here, and I can also have trousers, etc., dry-cleaned for hardly any money at all. I've had no trouble getting everything back, but Tek, who's had decidedly bad luck on this journey, (1) left the jacket of his most expensive suit behind in Moscow, and has received no answer to his letters to Moscow; (2) has got some kind of paint spot on the trousers of his second-best suit, which cannot be got rid of in any way, and (3) to his dismay, he still hasn't received back the whole suit he sent off for dry cleaning weeks ago. The boys from the hotel profess to know nothing about it. But now and then we buy a jug of *Maotai* (a kind of Chinese gin, quite drinkable), and then he cheers up for a while.

I'm taking photos at random, and have also bought a few series of slides; I've got almost 500 pictures in total. Tek's also started to take photos, but he doesn't know how his camera works – I hope that it's not all in vain! I'm seeing a lot of Roland, including at the 'Mandarin Club': every 14 days, 15-20 Chinese speakers (both Westerners and Chinese, including my tutor, Wu) meet, have an extensive meal, and talk about or show films and slides of journeys through China. The meeting is held exclusively in Chinese; some foreigners, such as the Englishman Wilson and the Indian Rama, speak incredibly well. My Chinese is improving, but it's still a question of getting by. This evening we had dinner at Laboyrie's, and tomorrow morning, with Roland and my Chinese tutor Xu, we will make a trek along the city walls and gates of Peking, which Xu has studied in depth.

In the diary, Erik devoted a long passage to this trek:

24 October

Lesson with Xu in the morning. We talked about the city walls and gates of Peking, which he has studied in depth using modern methods that he developed himself (for example, dating sections by measuring the building stones and the thickness of the layers of earth). He told me all about the measurements and sites in Peking during the Tang,[72] Liao-Jin,[73] Yuan and Ming eras. He collects photographs, would like to work with Roland on a large study of the walls and gates, and wants to give me a letter with corrections for Sirén. A fantastic well of knowledge. Evidently won over by my interest in the matter, he has promised to carve me a library seal with the text 'Helan Lihe Xushizhiyin' (seal of the collection of Mr. Xu Lihe from Holland) in small letters.

This afternoon, the four of us (with Roland and Xu) walked along the city walls and gates. A tiring walk, where we looked at everything closely. Terrible degradation of the walls and sad deterioration of the gates. If things go on like this, nothing will be left in a few years' time. The southern walls have disappeared completely, plus a large part of the eastern walls. Extensive digging is taking place on the other walls! Stone for temporary dwellings (site huts, barracks, et

---

72 The Tang dynasty ruled China between 618 and 907.
73 The Liao dynasty (also known as the Khitan Empire) ruled Northern China between 907 and 1125, and the Jin between 1115 and 1237.

cetera) and earth for construction. Depressing – in thirty years they will be kicking themselves![74]

It's slowly beginning to get damned cold here, and I'm seriously thinking about buying a sheepskin that I can wear as a <u>detachable</u> lining under my raincoat (at least, if I can fit something as thick as that underneath). They are widely available here, and cost 50-60 guilders. If we stay longer in the north, it's going to be a necessity. But what could I do with it after November? All problems that we're only going to be able to solve once we know something definitive, and this uncertainty is sometimes making us touchy. This afternoon I stayed at the hotel for the first time, because I feel like I've got a touch of flu, and the weather outside is chilly and foggy. Listed my slides, cleaned my shoes after walking through the dusty town, sewed on two buttons with true mastery, and took a warm bath – voluntarily, mind you (last time Tek drove me to it, under the pretext that he could 'smell me'). That story about the impossibility of getting a haircut in Peking is rubbish. There's a barber here at the hotel who, for the sum of 60 fen (= 0.90 guilders), will cut your hair beautifully, wash it, massage your scalp, and dry everything 'in style' with a dryer. Moreover, for 50 cents he'll give you such a perfect shave that your chin will still be smooth the next day. Tek's had two shaves purely for the sensation, even though he doesn't have a beard.

Until now, of course, we've not been able to see much beyond the city. Last Wednesday (21 October), evidently as a great exception, we were given permission to visit Zhoukoudian, ± 50 kilometres to the south-west of Peking – the location of the cave in which the remains of the Peking Man (Sinanthropus) were found, and where there is also a small museum with fossilized bones and

---

74 The city walls were torn down for the construction of the Beijing metro. Indeed, of the 40 kilometres of city walls, only 1.5 kilometres are now left. That a few monumental gates and corner towers are left is due to the fact that the demolition was halted after Mao's death in 1979.

bits of rock. Not particularly interesting for us, but the journey by car through farmland was very pleasant. Quite prosperous, on the whole; the harvest seems to be excellent. Whitewashed farmers' houses, quite a lot of industry (in the form of communes), and heavy traffic of donkey and ox carts along the roads.

It's incredibly densely populated, wherever you go – at least as densely populated as Western Holland. Even the smallest strip of ground has been cultivated (now mostly planted with winter cereal). There is no mechanization to be seen; it seems that all the agricultural work is done by hand, by enormous teams of men, women and children. You see large groups of school children working in the fields (in their free time, or as scouts), and you also see them weeding parks. This morning we saw one hundred children ('pioneers' with red neckscarves) in the large forecourt of the Imperial Palace, systematically weeding out the grass between the stones right across the whole enormous square. A massive collective undertaking, whereas we'd probably send one guy with a spray to kill the grass. And that's what you see everywhere: many hands at work, while even a vacuum cleaner is an unknown quantity. And at the same time (when considered necessary), there are hyper-modern electron microscopes, computers and an atomic bomb. That contrast makes China unique, I believe.

Although there is still so much to see, the isolation that comes, for example, from reading hardly any newspaper, and thus having no idea what is happening beyond China, does make one feel lonely. Today one month has passed, and sometimes I wonder whether I shall feel so good after three months in China. I am glad that Tek and I are here together (even if he sometimes goes on too much, especially early in the mornings); sometimes we sit for an hour, chatting about Leiden, Pott[75] and Ouwehand[76]-

75   Pieter Hendrik Pott (1918-1989), India curator and then director (1955-1981) of the National Museum of Ethnology in Leiden.
76   Cornelis Ouwehand (1920-1996), anthropologist and Tek's colleague as the curator of the Japanese collection at the National Museum of Ethonology.

with-the-nose, in some café or another as though it were the *Turk*.[77]

Dear Puck, it's become another muddled letter, 'written prematurely' and thus with very little news. But I'm writing when I get the chance – that's nicest for both of us! (I'll write again on Sunday – a short letter to tell you about dinner at Laboyrie's and the journey with Roland.) Bye, darling Puck and Erik-Jan, lots of love from your far-away and rather sniffly Eerft.

Letter 6: Beijing, 25 October

Dear Puck,

As promised, I'm writing another short letter this evening, despite having written a more detailed account the day before yesterday (Friday). What's more, this morning I got your last letter, dated 18 October, and Erik-Jan's (which I shall shortly honour with a lovely postcard in return). It's nice that Gwat & Hans Wams invited you; so you're still having a fun outing every now and then.

Michele's[78] inquiries as to how I'm doing could indeed have been accompanied by an invitation, but you know that he doesn't think of such things. Do your best on the circle's committee,[79] and above all, make sure that I'm spared from giving lectures for the time being. I'll first need a couple of month's breather in Holland! Although I think I'm going to limit the lectures in future; if the various adult education centres, societies for the common good and sailors'

77   A reference to the well-known restaurant in Leiden called 'In den Vergulden Turk [The gilded Turk],' which was situated on the Breestraat between 1900 and 1962, and then opposite the entrance to the National Museum of Ethnology (where the Institute of Sinology was also situated).

78   Michele Ondei: along with Tek, Erik's oldest friend from university. A Tibetologist and curator at the National Museum of Ethnology in Rotterdam (which later became the Wereldmuseum). He was also a novelist.

79   The 'circle' on whose committee Hanny sat was Leiden University's Association of Partners of Professors and Lectors. This club still existed in 2015 and Henny/Puck remained a member her entire life.

clubs and so on hear that I've returned from China with a couple of hundred slides, they'll probably be on my back – and you can count me out.

I've received letters from San and Kitty, and in Kitty's letter I could also sense tension and nerves. But to get cross about that remark I made is far-fetched. When I wrote that Holland was far away and that nothing here reminded me of Holland, I simply meant (as any neutral person would agree) that the Chinese surroundings differ from those in Holland in every respect, so there are no associations here with our familiar environment. If one wants to insist that this means 'we are so absorbed in a different world that we never think of you,' or something similar, then it's a question of splitting hairs. I had a go at Tek, by the way, because he hasn't been in touch with anyone yet, and his remark about Kitty's children (who wouldn't stand out here) was probably very tactless. (But, after all, it's true! Not only in a physical sense. Chinese children are dreadful and the parents let them do as they please. Wu Yixin showed us his beautiful collection of jade, kept in wonderful boxes lined with white satin. His two piglets of grandchildren, aged 6 and 8, climbed all over his knees and rubbed their grubby trotters all over the satin, making dirty smears and spots. And Yixin simply kept saying: 'Come on, Xiaofu, don't do that … come now … please don't do that!', et cetera.)

I have little news to report since last Friday. The dinner at the *Chargé d'Affaires'*, attended by a number of bigwigs, was nice to the extent that such things can be nice. I was sitting between the guest of honour, Junior Minister of Foreign Affairs Huan Xiang, and the chairman of the Europe section of the Organization for International Cultural Relations. In passing and in very general terms, I again brought up the matter of the length of our stay and our travel programme. It now appears that everything is being sorted out and that we will certainly be able to stay in China for around three months, if not longer.

Erik's expression of his displeasure earlier had evidently done its work; although the travel programme was not the only topic of the conversation, according to the diary:

23 October
Dinner went well. Two tables; I sat between Junior Minister Huan Xiang (around sixty years old, studied in England before the war, former Chinese ambassador in London for eight years, and a Miao, would you believe!)[80] and Mr. Wen from the Organization for International Cultural Relations, plus interpreter. Had a rather halting conversation with him about abstract art.

After dinner, to round off the evening, Roland showed two films he had made during his last diplomatic trip to the interior; very nice and beautiful colours.

Yesterday we took the car with Xu (one of my tutors) and Roland to make a trek along the walls and city gates of Peking, which Xu has studied in depth. Very impressive – but it's rather a shame that today's leaders don't share this opinion. For the ancient walls (14th-17th century, sometimes 26 metres thick) are being knocked down at a fast rate; the stones are being used for temporary barracks and site huts and then discarded, and the exterior tamped-down earth is constantly being transported to construction sites in lorries. Xu says pessimistically that in five or six years' time, all of the walls and gates will have disappeared. An incomprehensible act of vandalism; they will be kicking themselves in thirty years' time.

And it was not only the city's walls that were disappearing:

80   One of the officially recognized minorities in China; in fact, a group of peoples in Southern China and Indochina who call themselves the Hmong.

26 October

In today's paper: a resolute end is to be made to all 'super-stitious and feudal inscriptions' (*duilian*) on pharmacies, grocery stores, et cetera. They are to be replaced with healthy and stimulating social slogans. *Prosit.*[81] Many things are disappearing; I'm glad that I am able to see things now, because in ten years' time, China will have become utterly impersonal.

Other than that, we visited a few temples of mediocre quality today. It's already quite cold, but I've borrowed a thick winter coat from Roland that fits me rather well. Nevertheless, I seem to have caught a stubborn cold – a persistent cough, and that damned itching on my legs is back. Now it can't be a matter of diet, so it must be the dryness caused by the central heating. And I don't have my miracle cream with me!

Dearest Puck – I'm feeling quite homesick, although I express it differently from little Erik-Jan. I'm almost constantly weighed down by the strange atmosphere here and the absence of anything that's dear and familiar, and my mood is not improving. But I'm counting the days. Now I've been away for one-and-a-half months, so we're past a quarter of the way. Just grit the teeth and keep on writing! Although it is interesting to be here, I will be extremely glad to make the return journey in the spring, back home and back to you both. Until the next letter, lots and lots of love and kisses from Eerft.

Letter 7: Beijing, 29 October

Dear Puck,

Today's Thursday, but I'm writing already because we received a definitive answer from Luxingshe this morning. The length of our stay has now been fixed at three months, thus until 23 December. There

---

81   Translator's note: this expression means 'Your health' or 'Here's to you'.

may still be a few very small changes to our travel programme, but things are now pretty fixed. So I'm rushing to keep you up to date, also with an eye to writing letters. The programme now looks like this:

2 November	Leave Peking for Xi'an, perhaps also Luoyang, c. 1,200 km inland (we managed this with the help of the Cultural Organization and Roland)
3-7 November	In Xi'an and Luoyang
8 November	Back to Peking
9 November	Arrival in Peking
10-17 November	Last stay in Peking. We won't be staying in this hotel any longer, but in the more centrally located Xinqiao Hotel, Wangfu dajie. I don't know the room number yet. You could just write to the hotel, or you could simply keep writing to Minzu Fandian Room No. 518, and your letters will be picked up by Luxingshe and given to me.
18 November	Leave Peking by train for Nanjing
19 November	Arrival in Nanjing
20-23 November	Nanjing, also visit a few places outside the city
24 November	Leave Nanjing for Suzhou
25-28 November	Stay in Suzhou, visit Jingdezhen (porcelain kilns)
29 November	Leave Suzhou for Shanghai
30 November – 6 December	Stay in Shanghai
7 December	Leave Shanghai-Hangzhou
8-12 December	Stay in Hangzhou
13 December	Leave Hangzhou for Canton
14 December	In train
15 December	Arrival in Canton

| 16-22 December | Stay in Canton and surroundings |
| 24 December | Leave Canton, cross border to Hong Kong at Shenzhen |

When we're in Canton, we can reserve hotel rooms in Hong Kong via Luxingshe; we've just extended our visa for Hong Kong at the British embassy; the visa is now valid until 29 January, enough for one month's stay. Then I'll go to Japan for around three weeks (possibly accompanied by Tek, possibly alone), so until ± 15-18 February, and then I'll travel down to Cairo via New Delhi. I'll probably still be able to pay for the month in Hong Kong with the money from the ZWO, so don't transfer anything to Hong Kong for the time being. I'll be sure to let you know, possibly by telegram in an emergency.

As the journey to Xi'an is going ahead after all, we've got lots to do: packing, giving Roland rolls of film, sending off and packing up all kinds of things, etc. Just this morning, I had the books that I've bought here over the last five weeks (some for myself, some for the institute) packed and sent to our home address; they won't arrive for a month or so (all registered post). A total of 37 volumes and parts, including 19 volumes in Chinese, and the rest in English and French. There are also a number of books from the institute that I brought with me in September (Chinese textbooks, etc.), which I won't need any more.

Other than that, I've had a number of things sent to the museum with Tek's stuff; they'll remain packed until he comes back in July. Then I'll extract my things from the mass of objects, more than 350 of them, which he's bought here. Just in case (should I lose my notes), here's the list:

1 wooden brush tray; 1 inkstone in Nammu-wooden box; 1 stone box with Cinnabar; 1 stone seal carved by Wei Changqing; 2 porcelain tea cups with lid; 1 oxblood porcelain vase on a wooden stand; 1 'transformation'-glaze purple-red vase; four scrolls with calligraphy

and a large horizontal Chinese landscape (black and white) by Fu Songchuang.[82]

These are all things for us to keep, so there's no great hurry to open the parcels. I'll bring some smaller things (jade, a few small pieces of porcelain, some brocade, a fan, etc.) in my luggage.

Finally, today I'm also going to write to the ZWO (for the first time!), and will let Toon[83] know how the talks on the student exchange scheme are going. I also need to send a card to the Heestermans and to Ingrid, who still hasn't heard from me, and in time I should also ask Suzanne to find something for me in Kyoto (but on the other hand, perhaps I'd be better putting up in a hotel for those few weeks. Although a Dutchman who was here told me that Kyoto is prohibitively expensive: 40 guilders for a hotel room seems to be completely normal). So there's lots to do!

We haven't actually done very much recently (since Sunday, when I last wrote to you). We went to a 'modernized' Peking opera; the singing and acting were good, but it was still relatively kitsch owing to the forced 'socialist-realist' content, plus the lack of beautiful traditional theatrical costumes. Did I tell you that Tek spent an arm and a leg on such costumes? You're in for a treat, once he's displayed them in the museum! We spent much of Tuesday packing things up and sending off goods, and on Wednesday I made another short visit to Laboyrie, from whom I bought four tins of Nescafé, a large bottle of Bokma[84] and an assortment of 50 cigars for the sum of 15 yuan. So you see, a diplomatic representative can be useful! He's a kind man, but dulled by the diplomatic profession, and mainly interested in his years of service and pension.

Dearest Pucky, my apologies for this rather business-like letter – there's not been much else to report since Sunday. I'm really

82 Fu Songchuang (1913-1991). Better known as Puquan or Pu Songchuan. A twentieth-century painter and a nephew of Emperor Puyi (see note 116).

83 Hulsewé.

84 Translator's note: 'Bokma' is a brand of Dutch gin (*jenever*).

pleased that we're making progress, not least because it means that Hong Kong and Japan, and thus also Egypt, are coming into sight. To be honest, I'm already a bit fed up with Peking, although I don't complain too much to Tek. Will you write again soon? I'm always so happy to hear from you – it's really boring here without any news, in this expensive hotel. Lots and lots of love to you both and 10,000 kisses from Eerft.

PS: I received a letter from Father – he clearly hadn't received the letter that I wrote for Mother's birthday. The post is unreliable!

Letter 8: Beijing, 1 November

Dear Puck,

I'm writing to let you know that all's still well, although there's been little to report since 29 October, when I sent you my new travel programme, et cetera. Yesterday I received your letter dated 23 October (it took a week, but we should also allow for the extra time difference of around ten hours at Peking's expense, so it's really six days). It's wonderful that Erik-Jan's report is so good, and that he got such a good evaluation from Naeff.[85] With regard to winter sports, it's hard for me to advise you from here. It wouldn't be much fun to have to take care of Kitty's children. But what's the alternative? I thought that certain regions, such as Majorca, are still sunny even in December, but if that's not the case, then I wouldn't think it worth making such a big trip. Now I think that a winter sports holiday would be fun; in the evenings the children would be in bed, and during the day you could pack them off to the ice rink or suchlike. More important is the question of whether you can get on with Kitty over time if you're constantly together, however kind and easy-going she might be. I've noticed myself how difficult it can be

85   Jan Naeff, rector of the Rijnlands Lyceum Oegstgeest (a grammar school) between 1957 and 1970.

to maintain a good atmosphere with Tek, as we're together 14 or 15 hours a day. It only works if we're both prepared to compromise and if we don't attach too much importance to our own affairs. Tek has his moods, as do I, and the only solution is to take a humorous view of the other's bad mood. Things have gone pretty well so far, and we've already done over one-and-a-half months. So with a bit of good will, two weeks of winter sports wouldn't be too difficult. I'd go ahead and try – staying at home in December would be no fun, either.

I was aware that the Rijnlands Lyceum is a bourgeois little VVD[86] school, but what do you think the grammar school in Leiden is like (or, for that matter, our own Leiden University)? It's simply a fact that upper-secondary education is dominated by the middle classes. We must just ensure that Erik-Jan gets a healthy antidote at home to any reactionary rubbish that he might absorb at school. Luckily, he will be sensible (and stubborn) enough to form his own opinion as a teenager.

Regarding the journey to – and the stay in – Hong Kong: I don't know if it will be necessary to involve Bob Kramers.[87] Hotels are expensive, but they're not all in the Hilton class, and with the help of the people at the office of the *Chargé d'Affaires* here (who all regularly go to Hong Kong), I should be able to find a suitable place. Perhaps Bob could give me suggestions for renting an apartment, but I do wonder whether it's worth the effort for those ± four weeks. I would like to have the extra 3,400 guilders from the *Curatoren*[88] in reserve (for travel, and possibly for more serious things, as these can always happen) in the bank in Hong Kong (branch of the former

---

86 Translator's note: the VVD is the People's Part for Freedom and Democracy, a conservative-liberal political party in the Netherlands founded after the Second World War.

87 Robert Kramers (1920-2002). A sinologist who studied at Leiden University and was a professor in Zurich for many years.

88 Translator's note: the executive board of Leiden University.

Ned. Handel-Mij); could you have it transferred towards the end of the year?

Yes, the postage stamps here are really beautiful. A little too beautiful; it's actually impossible to get hold of normal ones! The Chinese deliberately speculate on the mania for collecting. There are at least ten series in circulation at a time, each larger and brighter than the next. In any case, one can get nice, colourful things everywhere, such as old embroidery, jade, woodcarvings, enamel, etc. All quite modern, made within the last century, but sometimes the traders aren't particularly fussy and we've been able to buy various things that are certainly of the best quality and not new. We'll also take a look around when we're in Xi'an and Canton; Roland, who's just returned from the annual trade fair in Canton, where he was sent as an observer, told me that there are still many antiques to be found. We'll also do our best to find something nice in Hong Kong, although we've been told that the prices in Hong Kong are a multiple (sometimes 8x) of those in Mainland China.

I've written a short report for the ZWO – it was high time. I didn't have much actual material to report for my so-called project, but that sort of thing can always be hidden artfully behind impressive sentences. I have written a letter to Toon about the more Sinological aspects and about student exchanges, which will presently become a real possibility. Otherwise, no striking events. Or rather: every day we see and experience something, but we've become so used to it that it doesn't make a great impression any more. Such as the entry of the King and Queen of Afghanistan into Peking yesterday, for example: the whole city centre was decorated with flags and banners, everywhere were rows of massed 'spontaneous' spectators with flowers, dance groups, choruses, et cetera. The procession passed our hotel, and as we're on the third floor I was able to watch everything and take a couple of photos (the weather was bad and dark that day). Earlier I became really irritated about the cynical way in which such 'spontaneous tributes' are staged down to the tiniest detail: little groups of people are shipped in hours beforehand; flowers and garlands are given out; the 'spectators', four rows deep, close off the road completely. Behind them (i.e. on the other side of the pavement) is a single, continuous row of officials, who keep the real pedestrians and spectators at a distance; not a single one person gets through the cordon. Perfect crowd management, but after a while it does become irritating.

Erik is even less sparing with his words in the diary:

Friday 30 October
This afternoon, the King and Queen of Afghanistan made their entrance. Disgusting spectacle. Music, drumming, singing, waving – and all for a feudal monarch who probably exploits his subjects even more than any colonial power.

My mood became even more wretched that day, because Luxingshe cheered us with the announcement that the travel costs (train and aeroplane) would <u>not</u> in fact be included in the famous 60 yuan a day. Kicked up a fuss with our guide, Ni; in the end, it luckily proved that the total travel costs were not so high after all; including Luoyang-Xi'an, around 200 yuan – but nevertheless, it's another setback to the tune of 300 guilders. And protesting won't help; reference is made to the 'regulations' and the matter is closed.

This afternoon, Tek and I again went to Tianqiao – the working-class entertainment district – a meeting place for storytellers, conjurers, acrobats, sword-fighters, shadow-players, et cetera. We saw some nice things (although the political transformation has already permeated very deeply. The storytellers still used the old narrative technique, with gestures, and accompanied on the drum and castanets, but the story is now about the heroic deeds of a member of the Communist party).

In recent days I've felt as though I've had a touch of flu, and this evening (it's now a quarter to eight) I'm going to let it run its course. If I'm not 100 per cent better tomorrow, I'll stay in bed in the morning. I don't want to risk going to Xi'an feeling shaky; that would be a crying shame.

Dearest Puck, it's become a three-page letter again, despite covering little. Life in Oegstgeest is boring, as you say; I do understand. Peking's not perfect, either. Despite there being so much to see, I'm longing for the two of you and the familiar feeling of home. Keep your spirits up during the gloomy days (here the weather is clear, but there's a dust storm), and just make the best of it.

Will you say hello to Erik-with-the-good-school-report for me? My next letter will probably be from Xi'an, Shanxi Province!! Bye-bye dear Puck, until the next letter, love and kisses from Eerft.

To Xi'an and Luoyang

On 3 November, Erik and Tek finally left for the interior, to visit the region known as the cradle of Chinese civilization. First, they flew to Xi'an. From the moment they arrived they undertook a series of trips and visits, many under the supervision of the guide they'd been assigned, Gao (who failed to impress Erik). The diary is full of observations and impressions, but Erik did not have time to write the next letter before they reached Luoyang.

3 November

Rose dreadfully early in the morning and set off for the airport; left at around half-past seven. Small aircraft with seats in rows of three and *very* small windows. Quite cloudy, but breaks in the cover every now and then, which we took advantage of (squatting in the side aisle by the small windows). The aircraft was also transporting a lot of cargo, a few soldiers with many family members, et cetera. The stewardess was a very young lady who spoke hardly a word of English. We taught her a few common expressions and gave her a pocket dictionary (after much protest). The view was very interesting: loess, terraced land, many reservoirs before Taiyuan, also tree plantations clearly visible as a grey-green haze on the mountains.

In Taiyuan we stopped for an hour at a tiny airfield in a freezing waiting room; then onwards. This is a loess region, so no more reservoirs. Taiyuan is situated in an enormous plain. We passed the Yellow River, which flows from here to the north-east; wonderfully wide and unbelievably yellow. Later, not far from Xi'an, we passed it again, this time where it bears away in a great curve from the north to the east.

Could see very clearly the place where the Wei and Yellow rivers merge.

Around 1 p.m. we landed successfully in Xi'an. We were met there by a polite Chinese, called Gao, so well-behaved and insignificant that we didn't even enquire as to his *ming* (forename). He doesn't speak a word of English, more or less Putunghoa with a Shanxi accent, quite difficult and hopeless for Tek (Tek is furious, he's sulking and wants to protest at length in Peking later).

We were immediately taken to the Renmin Daxia [hotel], a dreadful concrete edifice with 500 rooms, devoid of any character despite attempts at Chinese ornamentation and the monotonous wooden Chinese corner turrets on concrete bases. Originally built in 1953-57 for 'foreign experts' (you can guess who), but, said Gao, 'they left suddenly'. 'Yes, we know', we said, and nothing more had to be said.[89]

We got a first impression on the journey to the hotel. Strong (Ming) city walls, old *gulou* (drum tower) and *zhonglou* (clock tower), endless straight streets, relatively modern but otherwise quite boring and characterless. There is no heating at the hotel, for goodness' sake; it's freezing. Our protests make no difference (we were advised to wear lots of clothes and put lots of blankets on the bed!!). The rooms are spacious, but furnished dreadfully.

Gao arrived with the programme (somewhat culturally overloaded). In the afternoon (after a large and very good lunch), we were immediately taken to a museum (in an old Confucian temple), where we were shown round in truly unbearable fashion by two party know-it-alls, naturally

89   This refers to the rift between China and the Soviet Union in 1961, the 'Red Schism' that split the Communist world in two. All Russian consultants and technicians were expelled from the country.

preceded and followed by the official tea ceremony. In general, Peking has better pieces, with the exception of the *extremely* impressive colossal statues (including the remaining Tang Taizong horses).[90] The Beilin, the 'stele forest', is also here, including Han and later Stone Classics, the Nestorian stele of Xi'anfu, the famous portrait of Confucius, and so forth, many hundreds of them. We also saw rubbing work in process: the rubbing is made on sheets of paper that have been stuck to the stele and pushed forward with a brush. Eventually purchased a large rubbing.

Back to the hotel, where we ate a good meal and went to bed, desperate with exhaustion. The people here are different from in Peking; larger eyes, more squat, rustic and extremely friendly.

Wednesday 4 November

Early in the morning after breakfast, we went with that twit Gao to the tomb[91] of Qin Shi Huangdi.[92] Particularly interesting car journey (twenty kilometres or so) through loess landscape and ochre-yellow villages with some whitewashed houses, very neat and, as far as one can see, prosperous. As this is 'not a tourist area' I am not permitted to take a single photo, for goodness' sake. So I'm taking a careful look and remembering. It's striking that the farmers are well clad – better than the people in the cities, which are evidently not parasitical. Rather flat landscape. Ochre-yellow Behe River with broad mudflats and a new bridge. After driving for half an hour, saw Li Mountain in

90 Two horses. The other four were (and are) in a museum in Philadelphia.
91 That Erik doesn't say anything about the famous terracotta army that is displayed at this tomb is not a sign of nonchalance. When he was writing, the army had not yet been discovered (it would be found in 1974).
92 The first emperor of the Qin dynasty, ruled from 221-210 BC.

the distance, famous from historical accounts (site of the beacon tower of Zhou Youwang's bad-tempered Baosi).[93] We took a detour through a village with new streets and a levelled, tumbledown earth embankment, many small shops selling bazaar goods, and, would you believe it, a relatively large bookshop with communist literature. All along the road were wagons drawn by donkeys, mules, oxen and people (men, not women, mainly do the heavy work). Quite a few bicycles.

At the foot of the Lishan lies the Qinghua *gong*, once a spa town of the Ming Emperor Xuanzong and Yang Guifei,[94] fully 'restored'; that is to say, completely rebuilt in fancy Tang style, but a wonderful location with ponds and pavilions. Warm spring (43 degrees), the 'bath of Yang Guifei' is about as authentic as Volendam.[95] Very few tourists. Shown around by a pleasant girl. Historically, the most interesting thing was a small, genuine taoist temple fronted by 'iron flags'. Small courtyard, an altar with large statues of all kinds of gods and spirits, plus a complete set of paraphernalia, and in the courtyard there were two old taoists, eating. Our guides made over-loud, derisory remarks.

Followed by a long climb to the dreadful Greek-style memorial where Chiang Kai-shek was once taken prisoner by Zhang Xieliang, and Chiang's living quarters, from which

---

93   The story of the Beacon Tower, the watchtower (*Fenghuo Tai,*) is as follows: King You of the Zhou dynasty was married to Baosi, a beauty with a bad temper. In order to make her smile, the king made a habit of having the fire in the watchtower lit, whereby his vassals were put on alert for nothing. When the empire was attacked and the fire in the watchtower was lit with good reason, in the end not one vassal came to help the king. That was the end of the Western Zhou dynasty.

94   Yang Guifei (719-765), consort to the Tang Emperor Xuanzong.

95   Translator's note: a village in North Holland that has a reputation as a tourist trap.

he fled.[96] We were told an apocryphal story about Chiang's cowardice during the flight (a different version from the one we were told in Peking).

Long rest-pause before lunch, which I filled with a warm bath (in the so-called Ming Huang bathroom!), nice for the balls. Lunch in freezing hall, then went on to the tomb of Qin Shih Huangdi; it was massive, but there was little else to see (found a potsherd). There were Guomindang trenches in the *ling*.[97] Climbed to the top. Took various photos of a giant owl that was flying around. Bad, misty weather. Then to Banpocun,[98] which was particularly good and impressive. Shown round by an expert female archaeologist (plus dreadful party man). Looked at everything in detail, and in particular the covered site (around a seventh of the whole terrain, later excavated further). NB. I've promised to ask Leiden about a way to conserve this site, which will irrevocably crumble to bits).

At the end, the inevitable tea ceremony, with praise for the current flourishing of archaeology under the party's leadership[99] and, once again, the story of how art treasures were plundered by imperialists. I was critical of the demolition of the city walls of Peking. Tek was grumpy 'because I was too accommodating on the issue of art plundering,' but

96   Chiang (1887-1975), since 1927 the leader of the Guomindang (the Chinese Nationalist Party) and president of China, was involved in a bitter civil war with the Communist Party between 1927 and 1937 (and again after 1941). In December 1936 he was taken hostage by his own generals in Xi'an and forced to establish a common front with the Communists in the fight against Japan. After two weeks, he signed and the generals set him free.

97   Burial mound.

98   An excavated settlement from the Neolithic period.

99   The head of the state institute of archaeology at this time was Xia Nia (1910-1985), also known as 'the little Mao of archaeology'. Like Erik, Xia Nai began his studies as an Egyptologist.

I think because I was critical of the politics of demolition in Peking. Talk about hypocrisy!

Finally, went with Gao to see utter kitsch: the park with the *longchi* (dragon's pond), said to be Tang era, but actually a 100 per cent-new development with the exception of a single site with around ten bits of stone. There was a huge exhibition of chrysanthemums of every size, up to three metres tall. Returned to the city, which is rather boring, despite its large size and number of residents (one-and-a-half million!).[100]

In the evening, we went to a modern *yingxi*. Peking opera, Xi'an-style: *Ludanghuozhong* again,[101] with local players, Shanxi pronunciation and Shanxi music and singing, which I find more melodious than that in Peking. Icy cold in the hall. Apathetic audience and no interval. Returned to the cold hotel. Went to bed without a drink.

Thursday 5 November
In the morning, as agreed, walked through the city with an uncomprehending and sulky Gao, took photos of everyday life, city walls, et cetera; Tek bought a few pots and a brush in *Baihuo gongsi* (department store). At one point, Gao began to protest: we prefer China's 'backward' aspects, meaning that we're giving a false impression. I tried to convey to him what it's all about – successfully, I hope – but we won't be visiting the poorest neighbourhoods near the northern city wall. It's not necessary, either.

100   Forty-five years later in 2010, Xi'an (which used to be known as Sian) had 8.5 million residents.
101   *Ludang huzhong*: A spark in the reed-lands. One of the 'model operas' developed in the early 1960s by Jiang Qing, Mao's wife, as an example of a revolutionary form of Peking opera (with proletarian heroes). It is thus no coincidence that Erik and Tek were shown this opera.

In the afternoon, went to the *Maqisai renmin gongshe*, a people's commune six kilometres to the north of Xi'an. Made an extensive visit after explanation and introduction from the head of the commune, Fu (nice man). Among other things, we visited the *qianjing* (shallow well, 25 metres), the buildings of one production brigade (*Xianfeng shengchan-dui*, the 'vanguard production brigade'), namely the main street (of what used to be the village, later a single *Gao hezuoshe* or 'higher cooperative', still later a single production brigade in a commune).[102] Medical department with pharmacy and acupuncturist, primary school behind the medical department (applause as I entered), reading room, residential house belonging to a 77-year-old woman, and another house (both had two rooms; question: where do the children sleep?). There are 400 *Hu*[103] in this production brigade and the whole commune has 10,500 members. Then *hezongbu*[104] for general services, namely cowsheds and food products (noodles and tofu). Dutch cows that have been crossbred with Chinese ones. Then saw a deep well, 260 metres deep, with a 400-HP motor from Shanghai and a tank for directing the water so that it irrigates the land in different directions. Finally, visited one of the schools, the 'Agricultural Secondary School', with classroom and pupils playing basketball. Everything very neat and extremely well kept. They seem to have good prospects. According to Gao, this is a 'medium-sized commune.'

---

102 Former villages became independent 'production brigades' after the Communists came to power. The production brigades contained cooperatives made up of one or more streets. During the Great Leap Forwards, the production brigades were merged into much larger communes.
103 *Hu*: families.
104 *Hezongbu*: headquarters.

In the evening, we went to a melodramatic play in Qinqiang style, called *Nanfan nuhuo*, about the resistance struggle in Vietnam, with pointy-nosed red-haired Americans (and a caricature of an American lady). Wonderfully moving and not particularly subtle, but the singing and music were alright. Our isolation (and/or veneration as important guests) is complete: we arrived by car through a separate entrance, were met by leaders of the *Gongren julebu*[105] where it was held and were dumped in the first row, flanked by officials who had empty chairs beside them. Ritual as when the queen attends a performance, but we didn't enjoy it so much. As always, hall unheated, we freezing cold.

Saturday 7 November

In the morning made a quick trip to Ci'ensi, south of Xi'an (but originally within the walls of Tang Chang'an). Saw the monastery there and the Goose Pagoda.[106] Originally the monastery of Xuanzang,[107] but current building is no earlier than Ming. It is becoming increasingly evident that China has very few truly old buildings. To date, we have not seen one construction that is earlier than Yuan, and even those are incredibly rare.

Then to the station, part of the pre-war Longhai railway. Various stations are evidently from the Guomindang time;

---

105 *Gonren julebu*: workers' club.

106 The Pagoda of the Great Wild Goose is the most famous temple in Xi'an. It was built as early as 589 and known as the Wu Lou Si Temple. It was only completed in 652, during the Tang dynasty.

107 Buddhist monk and scholar from the seventh century, celebrated for his pilgrimage to India and the monumental report on his journey that he made for the Chinese emperor. For many centuries, this was the most comprehensive description of Central Asia. Naturally, for Erik, a specialist in early Chinese Buddhism, this was interesting.

along this railway line, they are built in a bizarre palace style.[108]

[In train] meals were plentiful, we weren't hungry. Train personnel clearly concerned about this; after the evening meal, much of which we left, the train conductor came to us with an 'opinions book.' He clearly thought that we had a low opinion of the food, and was annoyed. We did our best to reassure him. Tek gave me a lecture on Chinese niceties of action and reaction. I shall never get it.

In Luoyang, we were met by Mr. Li of Luxingshe. Seems nice and decent, but doesn't speak a word of English. His Chinese is not altogether standard and quite indistinct. According to him, there's nothing to see in Luoyang; everything in the city itself was destroyed during the war (something that tallies with Roland's reports). Provisional programme for tomorrow: in the morning we're to go to Longmen[109] and the museum (no guided tour), in the afternoon Han tombs and Baimasi. Quite enough for one day!

Sunday 8 November
In the morning at 8.30 a.m., went to Longmen with Li (polite young man, but speaks quickly and inarticulately, with *bubiaozhun*[110] pronunciation). Like everywhere in China, on the roads one sees huge numbers of carts piled with manure, wood, stones et cetera et cetera, pulled by people of all descriptions. Just beyond the bridge, the Longmen

---

108 The Longhai railway is the most important East-West railway in China. It was constructed at the beginning of the twentieth century by the Belgians, and later extended with money from Belgian and Dutch investors. The Guomindang, in turn, extended the railway in the 1930s and 1940s.

109 Complex of caves full of Buddhas, pagodas and inscriptions that were carved out of a thick stratum of limestone over six centuries.

110 *Bubiaozhun*: non-standard.

'site' begins. Countless niches, ninety per cent of which have been destroyed due to Chinese persecution and Western touristic and commercial vandalism. Inevitable welcome with tea from Mr. Hu, who gave us the usual story and then showed us around in unbearable fashion (like a worn-out tour guide). This largely spoiled the pleasure of looking around. Countless Chinese tourists gathered and watched us. But very impressive all the same. The site is now well looked-after and it is more open than in the past (people used to be brought by boat to the caves and then had to clamber over slippery stones). Those statues that have not been destroyed are wonderful, but in fact, only the very largest remain. The destruction is appalling and disgraceful. Water drips in through the stone (there's been a lot of rain recently), and in certain niches the water is at least ten centimetres deep.

Then to the museum in Luoyang, housed in the old *Guandi miao*, the largest Guandi temple in China, for its tomb (originally without a head, which was struck off by Sun Ch'uan and 'sent on' later). Wonderful collection of bronzes and pottery. Upon much insistence, supervised by surly and 'like-it-or-not' taciturn guide. Wonderfully peaceful.

After lunch, went from Luoyang to Baimasi.[111] Luoyang's old city was largely destroyed before and during the liberation; it's a small provincial city without any important buildings. A rustic character, like a succession of village streets; narrow and whitewashed houses, chickens in the street, et cetera. Back in 1949, not one street was paved.

---

111   The Temple of the White Horse. Considered the most ancient Buddhist temple in China, founded in 68 AD. For Erik, this would have been an emotional *lieu de mémoire*, but this does not come over in the diary.

Shops are modest, although not un-picturesque, but we didn't seem to be missing much.

At Baimasi we again went through the usual farce, with an abbot in a black robe and wearing a kind of black chef's hat, going on sanctimoniously about the blessings of the new regime.

Finally, went to a museum with a huge gallery full of tomb inscriptions from the Bei Wei, Sui and Tang. Three tombs have been transported in their entirety: one of Xi Han, one of Dong Han and one of Xi Jin. Saw the first two; particularly interesting, mainly due to exceptionally well-preserved paintings. Throngs of children followed us in the tomb and out again to the car. Drove away waving. Back to hotel though new Luoyang: straight factory sites; a large strip of green behind to the left, 200 metres wide, with the workers' compounds, and the 'shopping area' behind them (markets, et cetera). The whole thing was impressive. Among other things, drove past the large tractor factory (the largest in Asia) with 25,000 workers and annual production of 15,000 units. Our guesthouse is on the edge of this new city, not actually so isolated. Old Luoyang has become a rustic and insignificant appendage to this large new conurbation (many times larger than the old city).

At the hotel, dined with Li once more, very delicious and also brief. Tek wasn't feeling so well – he had a touch of flu and went to bed for a bit. I made my excuses and the meal was over quickly. Off to the train at 9:15. Back to Peking!

Letter 9: Luoyang, 9 November
Dear Puck,
I'm 'grabbing a second' to start this letter in Luoyang, in the half-hour that we're free between lunch and visiting the famous Baima

temple. Perhaps I'll be able to finish the letter today, otherwise I'll finish it early tomorrow morning when we're back in Peking.

We've almost completed our first major trip: by plane from Peking to Xi'an, four days in Xi'an, and yesterday by train (ten hours) to Luoyang, where we arrived yesterday evening. Once again we're staying in a massive 'hostel', no doubt originally built for Russian experts. The place is still called *Youyi* ('friendship'), but the Russian friends have long departed. One can see that here, too, those friends were not exactly prepared to live on the same level as the general population. For I'm sitting here in a suite that consists of a spacious salon with a sofa and armchairs, a large bedroom, a dining room, a kitchen and a large bathroom with WC, all lavishly furnished (by Chinese standards, at least), complete with central heating, telephone, radio and a view onto a large garden with a fountain and tennis court. When you think how the population, including its leaders, lives here, you can imagine that this created some resentment. The Chinese response appears to have been: let's isolate these essential but demanding lodgers. In both Xi'an and in Luoyang, the 'experts' residences' are located far from the centre (here in Luoyang, even around five kilometres beyond the city) in a kind of park, meaning that one sees only trees from the outside, and without any bus connection to the civilized world. The Russians constantly complained about the isolation, and I can well imagine why. It's OK for a few days, but over time it must be frustrating. There's massive board on the wall of the dining hall that has been covered over. What used to be underneath is anyone's guess.

As far as our trip is concerned, we can't complain about the quantity of things that we've seen. In Xi'an, the things that we wanted to see (such as the burial mound of Qin Shi Huangdi, the Maqisai people's commune, the Tang palace of Huaqingshan and the large textile factory) were located far from the city, so we were able see a great deal of the countryside during the car journeys. However, according to our guide (who was an incredibly silly twit), we were not permitted to take photos on the way. The situation in Peking was easier, and our guide here, too, is not particularly fussy. Nevertheless, I've got lots of interesting pictures, including a rather detailed series on the commune, which – as far as I know – has never been visited by European observers before. We were told that this is a medium-sized commune, thus not one of the largest or the best kind (we can't check whether this is true, of course). At any rate, it is impressive to see what they have achieved here on their own, with very few means. In order to irrigate the land, they drilled wells up to 300 metres deep (dug out with baskets, without drilling machines!); there was a medical department, a small pharmacist's, various schools, including an 'agricultural secondary school', a club with a library and a small cinema, etc. In the cowsheds there were cows that originally came from Holland; I greeted them as compatriots. The political indoctrination is 100 per cent, in every area and everywhere. Every wall has slogans and portraits; every book in the library and every song in the infant school has a political focus. At first sight it's oppressive, but strangely enough, after a month one gets quite immune to it. The people are probably so used to it they don't even notice it any more.

We're being treated in quite an obliging fashion. Mainly, I believe, because they've realized that we want to see modern things as well as ancient monuments. Some things, such as the large textile factory in Xi'an that we spent three-and-a-half hours visiting, are simply thrown into the deal. But it was actually interesting. Even though it was a model firm that had been carefully selected by Luxingshe, it remains a fact that it exists and it works! It was a splendid complex with thousands of workers (and their families, more than 20,000 people). We visited the whole factory, from the input of the raw cotton to the packaging of the woven material. Large machine halls with 3,200 thundering spinning and weaving machines (all Chinese-manufactured), with red flags for the record-breaking workers. Near the factory there is a true city, built by the workers and their families, with streets and squares, a club, a library, a department store, schools, nurseries, et cetera. The average wage is 50 yuan (75 guilders) a month (but it costs 8 mao = 1.20 guilders a month to rent a house, for example, and the prices in the department store are very low). Here, too, there is 100 per cent indoctrination. Every house has a larger-than-life-size portrait, you can guess of whom, and there are slogans wherever you look.

What's both interesting and tragicomic are the Buddhist temples that we are visiting here. To the extent that they are considered 'protected monuments', they are being looked after well by the current regime. But the monks who still live there and keep the worship going, to some extent, are in a strange position, one that becomes even stranger when a foreign busybody such as myself appears. We are usually shown around by the abbot, who first serves tea in a reception room (as happens everywhere), and then gives us a short tour. He tells us how miserable it was under the previous regime, and how good things are for them now, et cetera. Yesterday, the abbot of Ci'ensi in Xi'an declared proudly that he and his forty monks now formed a 'production team', and that during the 'Great Leap Forwards' they had achieved record harvests by working incredibly hard! All said with a wonderfully sanctimonious face and without moving a muscle. It's abundantly clear, of course, that the government is anti-religion, and in the temples (while the abbot is present) the guides speak of 'remnants of superstition from the feudal past.' And the abbot says nothing. The buildings are nice, but their contents (statues, paintings, et cetera) are worthless, almost without exception. The good pieces have gone to museums – rightly so, I believe, because the temple buildings are usually damp and unheated.

We had thought that we'd be able to buy some special things here, deep in the interior where there are hardly any tourists. But we've been disappointed – the fact that controls on art shops and antique dealers extend to the furthest corners of the empire is another indication of just how incredibly tight this regime's grip is. Shops are scarce and the wares have been combed through as efficiently as in Peking. That is to say, there are still some nice things for sale, but no real antiques such as Song porcelain or old paintings. In Xi'an, Tek again bought a number of bizarre objects, to the delight of the public (for example, two very small combs for combing one's beard and a knot of false hair of the sort used by balding old women), and I found a couple of small jade cups, polished very thin and the size of aperitif glasses, which can be used as such. Tek is walking around clad from head to toe in black leather and I'm still wearing Roland's old winter coat, which ends only 20 centimetres above my feet. Tek maintains that I'm the source of interest to the large crowds that constantly gather around us (with my pointy nose, blond hair and big feet), but I believe that he's attracting at least as many glances.

In the train we were treated with great courtesy, but we were isolated: we were asked when we would like to eat, and the dining car was neatly vacated at that time. Only the entire train staff (for whom our appearance is like a day out) sat in a wide circle around us for the whole meal, silently watching us and wondering how in god's name such people could exist.

Their courtesy knows no bounds, but it is combined with an almost pathological self-awareness, which expresses itself, for example, in refusing to accept anything, whatever it might be. At the station in Xi'an I accidentally sat on my pipe, breaking the stem. Maybe it could have been repaired, but there was no time for that, so I thought *soedah, laat maar*[112] and left it on the table. Shortly after the train left, the conductor presented me with the pieces of the pipe. I carefully explained that I no longer wanted the thing. 'Just leave it here in the ashtray,' he said. At the station in Luoyang the pieces were sent after me *again*. Then I gave them to

---

112   A Malaysian expression often used by Dutch people of East Indian origin. It means 'Enough, let it be'.

our guide, with the request that he throw them away. 'He couldn't do that', he said, 'without grounds for doing so.' So since then, I've been walking around with the bowl and stem in my pocket, and I'll probably have to carry them until we reach Hong Kong! And they went searching through the whole hotel for Tek so that they could repay him the single *fen* (1½ cents) that he had overpaid. Very decent – but it's the kind of honesty that conceals a high degree of pride and dogmatism. Matters are not taken lightly here; there is absolutely no flexibility, and there are the first signs of a fearsome bureaucracy. You should have seen how much difficulty we had trying to send a few books to Holland – as though it were a consignment of diamonds!

So there are nice things and annoying things, all mixed up together, something every day, so many things and so different that it is really impossible to say in a single sentence whether China's wonderful or not. On the whole we can get by here, although I long for you and for home in this sterile environment of hard work and obnoxious virtuousness. But it will presently be 15 November – and then I will have been away for two months, and a third of the time will be over. In two hours we'll go to the station, back to Peking (it's now 8 p.m.), where we'll stay for another week. Perhaps I'll find a letter from you waiting for me? I hope so – it's always such a treat to have your news. Goodbye, my dear darling, and say hello to Erik-Jan for me (and Tek says hello, too) – lots of love and kisses from Eerft.

From Beijing to Guangzhou

After their journey into the interior, Erik and Tek spent another week in Beijing. Before setting off again, they made a few last interesting visits.

12 November

In the morning, went to the *Fayuan si* monastery, shown around again by Zhou Shujia and by a monk called Zhengguo Fashi. Another largely Qing temple, Ming at best; aside from a few built-in inscriptions, none of the original Tang building remains; all that remains from the Liao era are two column bases. The museum inventory (statues, devotional objects, paintings, et cetera) was exhibited and almost everything was bullshit. At the end, over tea, Zhou Shujia explained that there were various 'classes', such as on the History of Buddhism in India, as well as in China and other countries, Japanese language, Pali, English (no French or Sanskrit), Abhidhamma,[113] et cetera. So it's a kind of Buddhist college, this Buddhist Association. Saw nothing of the library (there was one, in an outbuilding), only the Ming edition of the Tripitaka.[114] Xuanzang's skull relic (a piece of bone) in a little *cloisonné* pagoda on the altar in a special Xuanzang commemoration hall. The buildings were renovated in the 1950s. I didn't touch on doctrinal matters; embarrassing, especially due to the presence of two strange young men in Sun Yat-Sen uniform, one of whom studied 'Buddhist art' (the usual formula: 'the great works of the Chinese people', to be distinguished from 'superstition').

---

113 Third part of the Buddhist canon.
114 The three parts of the Buddhist canon.

13 November

In the morning went to Rongbaozhai, where we were met by Mme Feng. A painter herself and head of the block-printing department (set up in 1930 with four people, now more than one hundred). Under her supervision, observed the process of tracing, carving and printing. watched closely and took ten or twelve photos as documentation. Very pleasant people, promised to help Tek set up block-printing department at the museum.

14 November

At ten o'clock, the two of us went to Liulichang with Xu, very instructive. We gave Xu a little Yingshi[115] rock that used to form part of the collection of the brother of Puyi.[116] The shopkeeper was moved by this and found a fan that had belonged to the same man, for Tek to buy for the museum. Also a museum seal designed by Wei Changqing, and an inkstone and brushes. Took the stuff to Roland's; still need to collect it. Had lunch at Roland's. In the afternoon, we visited the city walls once more with him and Hsü, and also visited *Baita si* on the inside; very nice, lots of good, ancient *Thankas*[117] and good porcelain statues. The buildings are still largely early Ming. Statues around Kangxi – Qianlong. The temple is looked after by one old lama, otherwise deserted.

In the evening, dinner with Luxingshe, unfortunately; a waste of time.

115   A kind of limestone used in rock gardens.
116   Puyi (1906-1967) was the last emperor of China. He came to the throne aged two in 1908. The empire fell four years later, but Puyi continued to live in the Forbidden City until 1924. In 1964, on Mao's advice, he published his ghost-written memoires, which formed the basis for Bernardo Bertolucci's film *The Last Emperor*.
117   Colourful portrayal of Buddhist deities or scenes from Buddha's life, mostly made of painted paper stuck on silk.

Letter 10: Beijing, 14 November

(Tomorrow I will have been away for two months!)

Dear Puck,

Our final week in Peking is almost at an end! I hope that you received my letter from Luoyang; Roland told me that letters from the interior sometimes take weeks, because they're not used to such post and therefore first want to investigate and check everything. We arrived safely in Peking after an interesting train journey, with all kinds of experiences on the way. In our travel programme, the Luxingshe man had written: '1:55 arrival Peking'. Because he'd written down the other arrival and departure times as 13:20 and 16:45, and so on, we thought that we'd arrive at five to one in the morning.[118] So there we were, standing in the train in the middle of the night, all set to leave with our coats on, waiting at the door for the striking of the breaks, when an astonished and suspicious conductor spoke to us and asked us what we wanted. When we said that we wanted to get out in Peking, he said, phlegmatically: 'We won't be there for another twelve hours. Go back to sleep!' So we went back to our compartment, disappointed and freezing cold. The distances here are enormous: Xi'an-Peking is a total of 26 hours in the train, and if you look at the map you'll see that it's only a small part of China. We saw a lot of scenery on the way (although once again Tek slept loads) and I took lots of photos through the dusty window. I've already had 16 rolls of film developed (± 400 slides), and most of them have come out really nicely. We were rather isolated on the train. The conductor kept coming to ask us when we wanted to eat, and when we entered the dining car at the agreed time, it had been neatly cleared. The last few times we went a little earlier than agreed, to see how the diners were discretely and silently sent packing.

---

118 As we shall also see in the next letter, Erik had problems with travel times. Here he must have meant 'five to two'.

We're staying at the Xinqiao hotel in Peking. It's richly furnished and (aside from the food) better kept, and also more centrally situated, than the Minzu Fandian. From our rooms we have a splendid view of the Hatamen gate and the remaining part of the city wall. Otherwise there's very little news. It is great to be back in Peking, but the novelty has worn off, of course. We're doing some shopping and looking around, visiting a few things that we didn't see earlier or hadn't seen in full, and are saying farewell to various people.

It was a lovely surprise to get your letter dated 1 November, with all your news and questions, immediately on our return to Peking (Tuesday). I will write another card or letter to Frits[119] and Miyako tomorrow; it's really nice of them to invite you from time to time. Though Frits is not so bright and he is decidedly reactionary, in that respect he is certainly a good friend. I'm surprised by the news about Jan de Jong[120] and his possible emigration to Australia (traditionally a country of banished convicts). I'm still interested in Chinese Buddhism, of course; but I'm wondering, all things considered, whether it would be wise to aspire to the position if De Jong were to leave. In the first place, I would have to knuckle down seriously to Sanskrit, of which I know a little, and Tibetan, which I don't know any longer. That would take time and effort – perhaps years. And in the second place, I've now seen with my own eyes that Buddhism isn't playing a very meaningful role in the East any longer; what remains is a relic of the past, and I don't believe that there will be a revival. Perhaps my current field is too extensive, but it is a living one and it does offer possibilities for the future. So, *soedah laat maar*. Another question is who would succeed De Jong? Pott? He doesn't have any knowledge of oriental languages. Verwey? A nice guy, but just as passive and spineless as De Jong, although in a different way.

119 Frits Vos (1918-2000) and his spouse Miyako Kobayashi. As a Professor of Japanese, Vos had been Erik's colleague in Leiden since 1958.
120 Professor of Buddhology in Leiden. See the introduction for his relationship with Erik. De Jong was indeed appointed in Australia.

Sierksma[121] won't get a look-in, I hope, and heaven forbid we should get Hanna van Lohuizen, who, I believe, is keen to come to Leiden. We don't need to talk about Michele. Maybe the chair should remain vacant. But please don't let anyone expect me to take additional things on, or take responsibility for the Buddhology library; I've got enough on my plate already. But perhaps it's all idle rumour, so let's wait and see. Frits should concentrate for now on purchasing a washing machine and a Triumphcar, although he won't be able to beat Tek with his white Lancia! Such crazy excess only becomes really crazy once one's in a country like China, where the people save old crown caps and bent nails to be made into something else, and where one comes across bustling shops for second-hand screws. It never fails to astonish me how people manage to achieve great things by working with the most meagre resources.

Regarding my purchases: in addition to some small but fine works of art, I'm also still planning to bring some ordinary but nice everyday items with me. I mainly bought artistic objects in Peking, because Peking is by far the best place for that: jade, a few small pieces of porcelain, some embroidery, a seal with my name, a little Mongolian bowl made of silver and rosewood, and a few more knickknacks, either for us or to give away. There's such a huge amount available here, aside from the really old antiques, the really good ones of which are far beyond my means. There are also lots of nice everyday things: baskets, wickerwork, folk pottery, strings of beads, simple teapots made of rust-coloured Yixing earthenware, common porcelain, all kinds of furs, and so forth; and also rugs and quite good pieces of furniture (no older than 100 years). The great difficulty is transport. You have no idea how much trouble it causes even to send a parcel of books to Holland. Every item has to be inspected and packed by an official body, and numerous forms have

---

121 Fokke Sierksma (1917-1977), Freudian psychologist of religion. Lectured in Leiden and was also an essayist and poet.

to be filled in. It would be easier to take everything to the South myself, but wickerwork and simple pottery etc. are voluminous and breakable, to say nothing of rugs and furniture (rugs in any case are made to order, and are beautiful but not cheap: they start at 600-800 guilders for a small 1 x 2-metre rug). For that reason, I'll put off buying everyday items until we're in Canton; that is, in mid-December, just before we cross the border. Then I'll lug everything to Hong Kong, where I'll be able to ship things without any difficulty. Roland told me that there are lots of nice things of that sort on sale in Canton, unlike Hong Kong, where the market is fully geared towards tourists, with crazy prices. He saw a jade ring in Canton for 350 yuan (less than 500 guilders) and then saw an identical one in Hong Kong for 5,000 Hong Kong dollars; six times as much, in other words. Clothes and shoes and suchlike are apparently cheap in Hong Kong, particularly things like watches and binoculars, but I don't need those.

In any case, I'll do my best to buy nice things, and especially things that we can use. Ninety per cent of what's on sale in China is completely without any function: little pictures and thingummies and ivory tortoises, and so on; I can't appreciate such things at all, unlike Tek, who enjoys them and buys the most implausible objects.

How are your plans for the Christmas break going? I haven't heard from San & Kitty for a long time. Maybe it's hard to imagine how it can be here in China, looking forward to news from home. You shouldn't for a moment think that your letters aren't important because you don't have anything striking to report. Each letter is a joy to receive; even the most ordinary piece of news is so welcome! We're pretty much deprived of newspapers; sometimes we get a few old ones from Roland, but they come with the overland mail and are usually at least ten days old. The radio only plays Chinese arias and the same old news reports, of course.

Dear Puck, I'll be off to the South in two days' time, so I won't be getting a letter from you for a long time. Just write to E. ZURCHER

(FOREIGN TOURIST) C/O LUXINGSHE, CANTON, CHINA, then I'll get your letters in Canton via the travel bureau, but only after I've arrived in Canton, i.e. on 16 December. I'll keep writing from every city that we visit, of course – you've got our travel programme. It's going to be a tiresome, lonely month, without letters! Lots of love and kisses from Eerft (PS. If only I were home!)

PS: on Tuesday, when saying goodbye to Roland and Mieke, I gave Roland back the long woollen winter coat that I've been wearing for weeks. The temperature's just above freezing here, and sometimes it is sunny. But I've noticed that it's OK with sweaters and a raincoat. So don't worry about my suffering from the cold in China. In Canton it's 20 degrees and in Hong Kong 25!

Letter 11: Nanjing, 22 November
Dear Puck,

For the first time I'm writing a letter 'ins Blaue hinein', because we're on our way – and once we've reached Canton I'll find a letter from you (I hope). Until that time, we'll be wandering elusively through the centre and South of China. We've been away for some time, haven't we? Tomorrow we'll have been in China for two months; it feels like two years.

We left Peking safely, not without the usual ceremony and the inevitable complications. At the last minute, Tek managed to contact his old friend and penpal Wang Junming (spent ten years in America and is thus popularly known as 'Jimmy Wang'; an archaeologist in Peking and great chap). He persuaded us to spend an extra day in Peking and also to extend our stay in Nanjing to five days, as there's apparently so much to see there. You can imagine: Luxingshe was distraught, but we managed it all the same. And it was lucky we did, because that last day in Peking was the nicest of all. We're both interested in Peking opera, which, as you know, is on its way out. Through Roland, we'd made contact with a few Chinese 'fans' who knew of a place where a complete set of opera costumes was being kept, and where we could learn about the extremely complicated way in which such huge costumes are put on and how players are made up. This was very valuable, particularly because Tek had spent more than a thousand guilders on two costumes for the museum, which he wants to exhibit. Roland took us there and Mieke put herself at our disposal as a guinea pig (imagine – Mieke, whom we always thought rather stiff! She was 100 per cent better than expected. Really, she is very kind). In any case: Mieke was decked out as a 'heroine', I – in dreadful pain (as my buskins were much too small) – was dressed as the 'jeune premier', Roland was making a series of short recordings of the whole thing for the documentary, and Tek was furiously making notes. You should have seen it; you would have laughed yourself silly. But you'll get to see the photos in any case!

After our two Chinese tutors had had Peking's antiques dealers searching for a month, we finally succeeded in tracking down a real old bow and arrows – an extremely rare antique, and probably the last of its kind available. Roland is going to try to have it restored before having it sent to Holland, together with the 140 objects that Tek recently bought. For the time being, I've bought it for myself, but if needs be the museum will also be able to use it. When the bow and arrow arrived at the office of the Chargé d'Affaires, all the Chinese staff had a go at shooting with it (they hadn't seen such a thing in years), so that we had to go up ladders afterwards to pick the arrows out of the tree branches.[122]

In the evening, Tek and I gave a dinner of Peking duck in honour of Roland, Mieke and the tutors – a much-deserved thank-you for

122 It would have been better if Erik had managed this very rare purchase more discretely. The bow eventually fell under a Chinese export ban and never reached the Netherlands.

Erik in Peking opera costume.

everything they've done for us. Xu Shibai gave me a seal that he'd carved for me. The next morning on the train we were waved off by all the staff (including Ben and Saskia); a noisy farewell, surrounded by curious Chinese onlookers.

It's really a shame to leave Peking. After two months, we were starting to get used to it, getting to know people, et cetera. What's more, Peking is a city with a special atmosphere – something that 'old China hands', including Duyvendak, had always said, which I never really believed until I experienced it for myself. Peking and Paris, perhaps also Amsterdam, all have that special feeling that can't be put into words. Perhaps the right word is simply *gezellig*[123] – you feel nice and relaxed there, in some way or another. I'm afraid that the other Chinese cities are going to be less pleasant.

The train journey went well; it took around twelve hours on the train to Nanjing, where we arrived on the 20th, shortly after midday.[124] As usual, Tek slept around 80 per cent of the time on the way, and now he's cursing a sore throat, probably from the snoring. The hotel in Nanjing is situated some way from the centre, but it is peaceful and opulent. Nanjing doesn't have much to offer in an architectural sense; the city was almost completely destroyed in 1864, when the Taiping Rebellion was suppressed. The location is wonderful, though, on the unbelievably wide Yangzi, with fishermen's junks, and surrounded by low mountains covered with autumnal woods of red and yellow trees. Only now do I realize how absolutely huge this country is. Twelve hours in the train, and we're only half way up China. The night frost had begun in Peking and it was already bitterly cold; here, we walk around in our raincoats, flowers are still in bloom everywhere (chrysanthemums and even roses), and the roads are densely planted with sycamores, cypresses, agaves and even banana palm trees. Not only the plants, but also the whole

123 Translator's note: a Dutch word with no direct equivalent in English, *gezellig* can be translated as 'cosy', 'friendly', 'convivial' or 'enjoyable'.
124 This is puzzling. If, as Erik wrote, they had left Peking in the morning and had actually taken twelve hours, then they could never have arrived shortly after midday; at the earliest, they would have arrived at the end of the afternoon. Given that the distance is over 1,000 km, in the 1960s a train couldn't have taken much less than twelve hours to do this, so either the departure time or the time of arrival is incorrect.

atmosphere is sometimes strongly reminiscent of Southern France, enough to make one feel nostalgic. The streets also remind me a bit of Delhi, with their open-front shops and low white-washed houses in the side-streets. But the level of prosperity is much higher than in India – it's not a straightforward comparison. Naturally, I'm annoyed by the constant indoctrination, the never-ending slogans and portraits, and the plays and films that we have to see and that really make you sick. But, on the other hand, it is truly phenomenal what this government has done for the masses. I believe that even the most hardened conservative, had he a chance to see this, would be impressed. Once you've seen it, there can be no two ways about it: China has enormous potential and will develop into first-class world power in the coming twenty years. And the craziest thing is that there's hardly any evidence of true coercion (aside from a number of half-Westernized intellectuals, who are put under great pressure). The masses are 100-per-cent 'formed' and moulded by the new regime and are wholly prepared to support it.

Tek and I talk often about our impressions. Tek's background (as an overseas Chinese) is different from mine. I don't identify with the Chinese; I deliberately resist every tendency to identify, because I know how dangerous it can be, as shown by such uprooted spirits as Franke,[125] Mote[126] and Frits Vos. I do my best simply to register and note, with the usual criticism, which is sometimes fed by irritation. Tek has a tendency to identify, although it is very much the question whether the Chinese themselves consider him to be Chinese. I've heard from various sources that the overseas Chinese form a separate group in China, one that has (or is permitted) its own way of life

125 Here Erik is probably referring to Wolfgang Franke (1912-2007), a German Sinologist who was a professor in China from 1937. He married a Chinese woman. They returned to Germany in 1950, where he became a professor at Hamburg University.
126 Frederick Wade Mote (1922-2005), professor of Chinese history in Princeton between 1956 and 2000.

and that isolates itself from the rest, or is also isolated by the Chinese. Whatever the case, Tek is not very critical and feels a personal pride and satisfaction in seeing the new China (which is understandable), and in my opinion has an over-pronounced tendency to gloss over certain evident problems in a naïve manner. As a result, our conversation sometimes gets a bit tense and vitriolic, but luckily we both have thick skins, and after two months of daily interaction with each other you know roughly how far you can go. Incidentally, Tek is suffering almost physically from the fact that Chinese shopkeepers have mistaken him for a Japanese three times now.

Today we got hold of a list of hotels in Hong Kong (with prices). A great variety, and the prices are not to be sneezed at. One hotel even costs HK $ 570 per day (around 300 guilders). The cheap class ranges from twenty to forty guilders a day, hopefully including service and taxes (that's not indicated). I'll be OK with the money from the ZWO, but it will take significant chunk of my salary – around 2/3 of the total amount. I'll therefore ensure that I leave for Japan soon after 23 January (when the money from the ZWO runs out), where Suzanne will need to arrange cheap accommodation (Tek has decided not to come to Japan, so our ways will part in Hong Kong). Could you transfer the extra money from the *curatorium* to Hong Kong at the end of the December, as you wrote; then I'll be able to leave when I want to. I'll certainly buy some nice everyday items as well (such as particularly nice folk pottery), but I'd rather do that in Canton, due to transport problems. I'm really curious to find out where you'll go with Erik-Jan, now that the winter sports holiday isn't going ahead. In any case, make sure you do something fun! Don't spend the holidays fretting about the Dutch rain and wind. Couldn't you do a trip to Majorca, or perhaps Sicily? Take the money that's in the bank – it's worth it, and in Holland I'll earn it back with my 'lectures with slides.'

I've written a letter to Frits and Miyako, in which I thanked them once more for being so kind. I'll also write to San and Kitty again, although sadly I haven't heard from them for a long time. Am I not writing enough? Anyhow, now I must be patient until Canton, in almost four weeks.

Dearest darling, keep your spirits up. I think of you both so much and truly long for the journey home. What a moment it will be soon, at the airport in Cairo! Say hello to everyone for me, and also to our neighbours again – what I would give to watch a good international game.[127] I will write again from the next place (Suzhou).

Much love and kisses to you both, from Eerft/Pap.

PS. My blue suitcase is so full that it's starting to burst at the seams. I'm leaving my two pairs of long johns here, as I certainly won't be needing them. Sending them to Holland would create a huge administrative muddle and cost more than they're worth. And lugging them along with me wouldn't make sense, because I have to pay 25 guilders for every kilo of excess baggage. I will try to send other purchases (everyday items, et cetera) home by ship from Canton. Tek is having similar problems.

PS2 Just like Piet, I've been walking around for weeks with a Chinese lacquered umbrella. It's nice, but a dreadful thing to transport! I'm not allowed to send it 'due to the fire risk' and the bureaucrats here are worse than you could imagine.

Letter 12: Suzhou, 29 November
Dearest Puck,

Would you believe that I sometimes have the feeling that I'm living under water here? The last letter that I got from you (in Peking) is dated around 8 November, three weeks ago. There's nothing to be done about it, but being so completely isolated is starting to play on my nerves a bit. How might you and Erik-Jan be doing? Perhaps

127 Translator's note: here he is referring to football (the Dutch national team).

you've already discussed places for the Christmas holiday? Perhaps shocking things have happened? How are the various people in Leiden, the family and the neighbours doing? All questions that must remain unanswered for now. We also have no idea what's happening in the world. In Peking we'd sometimes get news from Roland, but here we don't get any news, aside from the Chinese press, which is 90 per cent rubbish or indigestible, at least for me. Anyhow, there's nothing to be done about it and I must wait until Canton, still another two weeks. (You do know that should there be an emergency, you can cable the Chargé d'Affaires, who can phone me anywhere via Luxingshe, but hopefully that won't be necessary!)

I wrote my last letter from Nanjing, where we have since seen all kinds of interesting and less interesting things. That's the way it is with the Luxingshe officials, true Chinese style; that's to say, it's a question of *tawarren*[128] and give-and-take. If we want to visit some old workshop or a ruined temple, OK, they concede to that, but then on the other hand we must visit a commune or a modern factory as well; a package deal, so to speak. Thus, for example, in Nanjing we wasted half a valuable morning on a lengthy visit to a wretched old building that housed the headquarters of the Communist delegation in 1947 during the peace negotiations with Chiang Kai-shek. Reminiscent of Catholicism, with all kinds of relics such as Zhou Enlai's straw hat, the leather bag belonging to (vice-president) Dong Biwu and all sorts of yellowing photographs. But the goodwill that you build by admiring such a wreck creates the opportunity to visit other things, which other 'tourists' certainly don't get to see. We've largely managed to avoid large modern state firms, which is where they prefer to take Western visitors. By contrast, we've made various visits to small workshops and factories where all kinds of old crafts are continued (sometimes purely by hand, sometimes half-mechanized): jade-cutting, woodworking, brocade and embroidery, a kiln

128 Malays expression meaning 'negotiating, bargaining'.

for folk porcelain (where I bought a few small bowls for the heck of it) and silk-weaving. Sometimes small businesses on the edge of the city or hidden in side streets. By taking a good look around, you not only learn a lot about the craft (which is more important for Tek than for me), but also about the working conditions, housing, safety measures at work, et cetera. Sometimes the managers try to pull the wool over our eyes, but in such a naïve way that it really doesn't work anymore. For example, when we visited a silk-weaving mill yesterday, the director led us through the large weaving hall, where around 600 automatic weaving looms were thundering, mainly operated by girls and women. Of course we walked through the hall between two rows of machines, from one side of the hall to the other. In that row only adorable girls were working, clad in colourful blouses of multi-coloured cloth (something you rarely see in the street, even on Sundays). By peering indiscreetly between the machines to the other rows, where the women were working dressed as usual in patched rough blue cloth and dirty overalls, I could see that we'd been taken for a ride in a naïve way, but luckily not very seriously. Because, whatever the case, all of the workers looked good, the building that housed this small factory was considerable, and the machines were safe (in the past, women would frequently be dragged between the unprotected cogs). Child labour has been eliminated in the cities. The youngest workers are gangly youths of around seventeen. The situation in the countryside is different (probably the case all over the world). There, you even see infants of around four dragging a bundle of hay, and yet smaller children crawling around in the fields or in the middle of the road while their mothers work.

We liked Nanjing, mainly for its unusually pleasant climate. We therefore went to Suzhou on the 26th, two days later than originally planned. What's more, the extension gave me an opportunity to do something for my 'show-project' for the ZWO; in the end, I must be able to say <u>something</u> in my report. So on the 25th I went to Nanjing

University, where the ZWO had arranged a discussion with the head of the historical department, the well-known old Prof. Han Rulin. It was a long and interesting discussion. For the first time, I got quite a detailed impression of the structure of the degree programme, including the political training and compulsory discussion and 'participation in productive labour.' The students are 'formed' one hundred per cent, spiritually and physically, and intellectually as well as politically and morally; this is openly admitted. In discussion groups, Mao's writings are discussed and explained letter for letter. Newspaper articles are analysed as though they were scientific documents. The students seem to have little time left for study (in our sense of the word), and it remains to be seen whether this won't have an impact in the long term. Old Han was a kind fellow – kinder than the silent woman who sat next to him and wrote down every word of the conversation. That's the way it is, and people have reconciled themselves to it completely. A private meeting or a real personal discussion is impossible. The control is complete and unerring.

The few people with whom we have had personal contact have been fringe figures, those hanging on to the edge of Chinese society: the Chinese tutors in Peking, interpreters at the embassies and Chinese from Indonesia who have come to live in China and who naturally all live together and isolate themselves. There is no lack of overseas Chinese here! They are in all the hotels, sometimes in groups of many dozens, shown around by smiling and exceptionally obliging guides. They bring in a great deal of money during their visits to their families, and the propaganda value of the enthusiastic travel stories they tell back in Malacca and Indonesia (or Holland) makes up, from the Chinese perspective, for the nuisance that they cause. For they are certainly a nuisance in the eyes of the common man, as they walk around, flaunting expensive suits, gold watches, expensive Leicas and filming equipment and so on (a bit like the filthy rich ex-Dutchman who comes to 'do' Holland after twenty years of living in America). Otherwise there are loads of Africans here, mostly dance groups and other cultural figures, often dressed in beautiful natural costume. Nice people, but incredibly noisy; singing over-loud songs in the dead of night. Finally, there are whole groups of Japanese businessmen and tourists, who are scouting the Chinese market. Although they'll be disappointed; at a small industrial show we visited in Nanjing, to our amazement we saw computers, small transistor appliances, electron microscopes and dozens of kinds of Nylon and Orlon, all recently manufactured in China. One shouldn't assume that Chinese citizens could buy these, though. All the best things are for export, to get money to invest in industry. The most splendid brocade is woven, and furniture is made from the most precious kinds of wood, but these are sold in Hong Kong and Japan and to foreigners as a favour in special 'friendship shops', with large boards outside announcing that access is for 'friends from abroad' only. The common man here will have to make do with his blue cotton and his bamboo chairs for some time to come (which are lovely, in any case, and dead cheap. But how to transport them?).

Now we are in Suzhou, famous for its gardens and parks.

They had already visited some of them, as the diary relates:

Friday 27 November
In the afternoon, went to the largest and most famous (Ming/Qing) garden, the Zhuozheng yuan, designed by two celebrated painters (Wang and Shen, which?), late Ming. Large and intricate; in my opinion messy and excessive, with a strong tendency towards the grotesque.

Saturday 28 November
In the afternoon, went by car to two scenic beauty spots south-west of Suzhou, namely Tianpingshan and Lingyanshan. Modern Buddha statues (post-1949) carved by

monks who are still alive today. From the top there are wonderful views of the region, in which the mountains lie like stranded boats (alluvial region, so mountains were originally islands), and on the other side Lake Taihu in the distance, where there is now a large monastery with more than one hundred monks (had lunch in restaurant annex run by monks). Lovely monastery, but Ming at the latest, of course.[129] The collection is extremely important however. True museum, mostly statues, from Liu Song to Qing. The guide explained that there is still quite a lot of worship; clear signs of burning incense.

Then Tianpinshan; wonderful 'mountain', really a rather small hill of huge boulders with numerous inscriptions, little pavilions, stone staircases, small bridges, et cetera. Including Yixiantian, a narrow crevice through which one has to squeeze as one goes up. Very idyllic and refined. On the way down we visited the famous spring and tearoom, where the waters are taken (in tea), with a view over the autumnal trees and the white temple at the foot. The temple is no longer in use, but parts can be visited as a site of interest. Among other things, hall with an inscription by the Manchu Emperor Qianlong, who was here too.

It's all very beautiful and idyllic, but as you know, I only feel at ease in a large city. There's a southern atmosphere: small whitewashed houses, lots of canals and canal-side streets with picturesque little boats, and here and there palm trees and even agaves. The temperature has dropped, though; around ten degrees, with quite a bitter wind. We're gradually entering those parts of China where dog, snake and giant lizard regularly appear on the menu. I want to try it, but it disgusts Tek and he asks the waiter what is in every meat dish.

129 Sic; should have been 'earliest'.

A dreadful fact: the dogs are put in the water alive and are literally boiled to death, because it is thought that the flesh becomes more tender as a result of the tormented animal's thrashing and writhing. The cruelty towards animals here is truly appalling. It is the only characteristic of the Chinese that I really cannot bear.

Tomorrow we go to Shanghai, the largest city in China (ten million inhabitants!) and the most Western, with skyscrapers and heavy traffic. A relief for me, after all the nature here!

But in Shanghaizou he was again confronted with cruelty to animals:

Friday 4 December
After lunch, I went to the waterfront and wandered around. Among other things, passed a market where a trader was flogging a kind of pin with a hook on it for catching mice and rats. He had fixed a live rat with a hook in its throat to his stall as a decoration, and was surrounded by a throng of amused spectators. The cruelty to animals is repulsive and deeply ingrained.

Although there was more of a focus on nature in Suzhou than Erik would have liked, there was also time for more urban entertainment. His knowledge and appreciation of Chinese music appeared to be growing.

Saturday 28 November
Back at the hotel for dinner in the evening, a kraut came up to me (a student of Herbert Franke,[130] met him at a conference in Breukelen): namely, Werner Burger. I hadn't

130 Herbert Franke (1914-2011). Leading German historian of China in post-war Germany and a professor in Munich.

recognized him. He and his wife are in Shanghai as teachers (she does ink cakes,[131] he does Chinese economic history), and asked whether we would come and visit. Telephone numbers and address. Prick of a guy, not keen on the idea.

Sunday 29 November
Then a short visit to a very large taoist temple. Still quite a lot of worship with burning incense, kowtowing[132] children, among other things. There are currently still around twenty priests there. Rounded off with an antiques shop near the temple, where I bought a splendid blue (Yixing?) pot for Y 8, surrounded by a huge crowd (certainly over a hundred hangers-on).

In the evening, went to an unusually interesting performance of Suzhou *Pingtan*[133] in local dialect, always three speakers/musicians at the same time, in three 'scenes'. Perfect technique and expression and at any rate, one of the female artists (Lu Qihong) had a fantastic, clear voice and beautiful delivery. Accompaniment (two *pipas* and one I-don't-know-what) was like hillbilly.

Dear Pucky, as I've already said: despite all the hustle and bustle, the loneliness is beginning to get me down. I am so looking forward to Canton and to the letter that is hopefully waiting for me there. I just hope that everything is OK with you both and that Erik-Jan's support and company are helping you through your loneliness. Alone is still

---

131   She studied the arrangement of and decorations on 'ink cakes', the sticks that scholars used to prepare their ink.
132   A deep, respectful bow, with one's forehead on the ground.
133   *Pingtan* is a form of prosimetric rhetoric: the story is told in alternating passages of (spoken) prose and (sung) rhyme. Such genres are to be found throughout China, but the *Pingtan* of Suzhou is the most famous.

alone! But seeing one other again will be all the more wonderful. Goodbye my darling, lots of kisses from Eerft

P.S. I shall send Erik-Jan a postcard from Shanghai tomorrow. Here in Suzhou there's clearly another round of retrenchment underway, because it's impossible to find any postcards!

Letter 13: Shanghai, 6 December

Dear Puck,
You should get this letter just before the fourteenth; hopefully it will be the only time that we spend our wedding anniversary so far apart! And it was the feast of St Nicholas yesterday; something one doesn't really notice in Shanghai, but a melancholy day for me, all the same. What did the two of you do? Did Mam come over or did you both go to De Bilt? And did St Nicholas play his part? My presents will have to wait until I'm back.

We've been in Shanghai for almost a week. An enormous city with big, Western buildings, mostly in pompous Victorian style, all dating back to the time when Shanghai was the heart of Western power. The new regime has taken over everything, but the old liveliness is gone, both in a good and in a bad sense. So on the one hand, there are no red light districts or opium dens any more, but on the other hand also no heavy traffic, no garish electric signs or expensive shops. The streets are mostly straight and wide, well-paved and certainly as large as the boulevards in Paris, but if you look carefully, every now and then you see a car driving in the distance, or a thirty-year-old tram. There are great teeming crowds of people and large department stores with escalators (not in use, so as to save electricity), well stocked with wares of at best mediocre quality. You can buy works of art, brocade, wonderful silk, etc. to your heart's desire, not only in normal antique shops, but also in the so-called 'Friendship Shop', especially for foreigners. According to the new rules, we can get a reduction there of 30-60 per cent (but the prices are high, much higher than in Peking). In general, one hardly sees any Chinese customers in the art and antique shops (even in the normal ones). Some pieces cost no more than a few guilders, but that is still beyond the purchasing power of the average citizen. It is very clear that this city has long experience of dealing with foreigners. Many shop staff speak English and the prices reflect the fact that the wares are aimed specifically at foreigners. The clothes are also very different. In Peking, almost everyone walks around dressed in dark-blue woven cloth, but here you see many people (mostly women and young girls) wearing colourful tunics and red or flower-print jackets, mostly quilted cotton, but sometimes wool, too. Wool is prohibitively expensive here and seldom worn. Good woollen cloth can easily cost around fifty guilders a metre. By contrast, tailoring is not expensive; for around sixty guilders, a tailor will make an excellent suit in two days. We can get such a good reduction on the woollen material, though, that a fitted suit of a high-quality material costs no more than around 120 guilders. Tek is having one made here of a quite vivid blue that I can't say I like. I think that I shall have a lightweight suit made in Canton, as the material here is a little too heavy for that.

Tuesday 1 December

Spent the whole morning at the Shanghai industry show. Countless industrial products in the giant and monstrous Russia-China house. Party bigwig Jiang came with us and made orthodox remarks, clearly the 'second man'. Yu, our guide, was very good. The exhibition was multifaceted and tiring, lathes and generators, et cetera. Tek explained the true nature of Jef Last's reports to the gentlemen;[134] fantastic.

134 Josephus Carel Franciscus Last (1898-1972). Radical socialist (and sometime Communist) writer, journalist and activist. Spent a year studying Chinese in Leiden in 1918, and took his doctorate in Hamburg in 1957 as a sinologist. Fiercely anti-colonialist, with a very high opinion of Communist China. In Erik's opinion, a

After lunch, went to a very interesting handicrafts centre. Shown around by the director (a party rat), who is himself a master paper-cutter. Various departments: woodcutting, ivory, ink stones, palace lanterns, artificial flowers, knitting, paper-cutting and clay figures, etc. At the wool-embroidery department, we saw a plum blossom 'painting' being made, inspired by a poem by Mao Zedong; in my opinion, a wonderful specimen! We were both presented with a paper-cutting and a paste figure; I shall give mine to the museum.

In the evening went to a neo-Shanghai-opera version of *Ludang huozhang*, extremely nationalistic (only the songs were still in traditional style, but they had also been modernized in places with choruses and duets, for example). Lively and very well done, a much more elaborate version that was also different in other ways (according to Prof. Yu, this opera began as the creation of this group and was later adopted by other companies in different local styles). Thus lots of variants, also in the text, just like classical drama. The staging (décor) was extremely naturalistic and technically brilliant (wading through water and actors in showers of rain, projected onto an incredibly thin, near-transparent gauze stage-curtain). This version was very long, from 7:15 p.m. until almost 11:00 p.m.

Here in Shanghai, we've experienced our baptism of fire as far as mass demonstrations are concerned. It seems that a Belgian-American intervention is underway in Congo;[135] I don't know all the ins and outs, because we have no access to readable newspapers. In

'fellow traveller'. The 'true nature' may refer to the homosexual elements of Last's work.

135 This concerned the counteroffensive by the pro-Western Congolese government against the Maoist-led Simba rebels, who had taken control of a large part of Eastern and Northern Congo in 1964.

any case: almost every day there are huge demonstrations, around 200,000 men and women marching through the streets with countless red flags, banners with slogans, cartoons on large placards and so forth. The pacesetters walk alongside the crowd and scream a slogan every thirty seconds, such as 'American imperialists, get the hell out of Congo' or 'Long Live Chinese-Congolese solidarity'. Sometimes they hold printed sheets showing the slogans in the right order, which they peek at from time to time. Everything is one hundred per cent staged and prepared, but the incredible crowds are impressive, nevertheless. It must be a heart-warming spectacle for the Congolese who are staying at our hotel (a dance group). The Congolese are difficult customers, by the way. They walk around whistling and singing, day and night. According to Tek, who, as you know, judges people with his nose, they give off an intolerable smell. I don't notice it at all, but I did catch a Chinese lift attendant spraying a lift with some kind of perfume spray, shortly after some Congolese had been in it.

The hotel is a Victorian colossus, full of shabby velvet and pompom trimming – another legacy of the half-colonial era. Our fellow guests are mainly 'overseas Chinese', Japanese, Congolese, Indonesians and Latin Americans (Cubans?).

Otherwise there's relatively little for us to see in this city, despite its size. The architecture is largely European, the shops are well-stocked but characterless, the plays we've seen are so modern they've lost their character, and the people's language gradually so different from Peking Chinese that we no longer even need make any effort to understand people.

Yesterday I went to the university here, to talk to a few people from the history department. Now, I say talk – naturally not a tête-à-tête, but in the company of the 100-per-cent dogmatic party man/president of the university and a few more people whose roles were not clear. I didn't get much out of the discussion, because three quarters of it was almost a word-for-word replica of the story I'd been told in Nanjing. It is always clear, however, that the specialists (that is, the real scholars, as compared to the real party stooges/ politicians who are their superiors) are genuinely delighted to receive such a visit and with the little contact they can get. They wear themselves out with courtesy and show you everything that they can. It's the case here, too, that the humanities faculty is the dupe. The laboratories that I was shown (full of dreadful apparatus, I have no idea what it all was) seemed decent, but the history department was housed in a musty, broken-down little building with cracked walls. Just like Leiden.

Saturday 5 December

In the afternoon, I went with Yu to the university, Fudan daxue. We were received by the dean and the head of the history faculty, Wang (later also a younger historian – of modern history?). Welcome and explanation like those in Nanjing, but here the dean even has a little book, crammed with writing, for inspiration on all kinds of subjects (sometimes word-for-word what Han Rulin told me in Nanjing). Fudin was founded in 1905 as a counterweight to the Catholic Université de l'Aurore. It has been extended many times since 1949, now has 5,000 students, twelve Xi[136] and a library with 1,200,000 volumes. I visited various laboratories where I didn't understand a thing (all kinds of machines, all 'manufactured here, without foreign assistance'), a collection of taxidermy, then a small and dilapidated history department (in an old wing); small library and locked room with pre-liberation ideological reading matter. By contrast, the other building had a study room for Mao's thought, nicely furnished and complete with large limestone bust.

136 Xi: departments.

The only thing that I've personally had enough of is Chinese food, strangely enough. In one way or another, I feel a sense of disgust when it's put on the table; all those bowls of fatty meat and fish, and those half-boiled vegetables in slimy fat, and that mess of soya and prawns… I just eat a few mouthfuls of this and that in order to stay healthy, otherwise I simply eat white rice. The Western food here is not good. Evidently, my Dutch nature is getting the better of me after all. I'm simply longing for a tender steak or a wonderful cutlet with peas. My God, what I would give to eat something like that. Not to mention liquorice or croquettes. People eat an unbelievable amount here. Food lies at the heart of everything, to the extent that it makes you feel nauseous. In every street there are several food shops, which, in addition to normal foodstuffs, also sell an incredible number of delicacies (more or less), such as dried and salted plums, candied figs, edible seeds, roasted chestnuts and so on (there are very few real sweets, but there are all kinds of cookies, cold ones and warm ones).

And dog, of course:

Sunday 20 December
In a shop, again looked at roasted doggy and drank coffee in a familiar *Penjing*[137] tent, with marching music blasting out in our honour.

Aside from their complete asexuality, the Chinese are the most physical people on earth. Life revolves around eating lots and eating well, sleeping soundly, taking nice, warm baths and, for the rest, burping, pissing, breaking wind et cetera *en plein public,* freely and with the greatest imaginable candour. Back in Xi'an, a sweet, nice

137 *Penjing*: bonsai. Here Erik was probably referring to a restaurant decorated with bonsai trees.

girl who was showing us around a museum fell silent during her explanation, did two substantial, loud farts, and then carried on with her explanation. And the most delightful little creatures hawk and spit copiously in the street, or blow their nose between two fingers; but so many countries, so many customs – the Chinese consider our blowing in tissues to be the most disgusting thing they could imagine!

Otherwise we've walked along the waterfront, and crossed the harbour by ferry. The harbour, one of the largest in the world, is just like the streets of the city – large and spacious, but with little traffic. A small ship here and there, but nothing compared to Rotterdam.[138]

I have bought a collection of five complete performances of Chinese opera in different styles for the institute. A treat for your ears when I get back! Perhaps it's Shanghai that's put me in a depressed mood. Perhaps it's the denial of all contact; this really must end soon, because to be honest, it's really getting me down. Tek isn't suffering like this, but in the end he's a singleton, to his great regret (he still hopes to find a wife here in the East, poor thing!).

Sunday 6 December
In the evening, alas, received phone call from Burger and wife. Went to their *dasha* in Shanghai for a while; huge barracks-like building at the northern end of the Bund. Had to fill in all kinds of forms in order to be let upstairs. Burger showed me books and pictures of coins (also my Central Asian coins late Qing, perhaps even time of Yaqub Beg).[139] Described the ups and downs of teaching. Textbook is trash with old nonsense and silly texts, mainly on China itself. On the other hand, Burger is coarse and tactless about

138 In 1964 Rotterdam was the busiest port in the world. Now Rotterdam has slipped to fifth place and Shanghai is the busiest port in the world.
139 Uzbek warlord who controlled large parts of Eastern Turkestan (Chinese Xinjiang) between 1865 and 1877.

the Chinese. His wife studies ink cakes, following Franke; Burger, economic history in the Qing period, specializing in coin statistics. Went home full of beer.

Monday 7 December
Endless lunch with Yu and Luxingshe manager Xuan, who spoke pedantically in stereotypes, naturally about China (every remark by Tek or myself about the situation in the West was received with total indifference; people do <u>not</u> want to hear about the West, dangerous mental isolation).

Tomorrow we're going to Hangzhou for around a week, and then to Canton. I am longing for a sign of life from you! Tell me about everything in detail. Even the most trivial everyday things are welcome news for me in which I immerse myself enthusiastically. For the time being, I can only gaze at your photos, in which I can also see San and Kitty and poor old Lodewijk[140] in the background. Will you also tell me about your plans for the Christmas vacation? Bye, dear Pucky, lots and lots of love to you both.
Kisses from Eerft

---

140 The family's short-lived and much-mourned smooth-haired dachshund.

Guangzhou and Hong Kong

Letter 14: Guangzhou, 13 December

Dear Puck,

As you can see, we arrived in Canton earlier than planned. In Hang-zhou it kept raining harder and harder, and the mist got so thick that we could hardly see the beautiful surroundings any more. So we decided to cut our stay short, which meant extra administrative fees, but anything would be better than to waste our precious days in China moping around in a hotel. So we spent the last day (10 December) visiting monuments glistening with rain and packing.

Thursday 10 December

In the afternoon, still raining, went to Fei lafeng, where we drank tea prepared with the famous spring water in what evidently used to be a large monastery. Dissolved minerals in the water give it an unusually high degree of surface tension: girl demonstrated convex surface raised up by coins that were thrown in, and finally even two coins floating on the water.

At 11 o'clock in the evening (the dead of night, by Chinese stand-ards), we boarded the train. Despite the draughtiness of the old carriage, the journey went well: 36 hours, thus roughly the journey from Amsterdam to Rome! The two of us usually have a compart-ment to ourselves, but this time the train was so full that we had company. Our fellow passenger was a railway engineer, a decent man who had previously studied in the US and Hamburg. We whiled away the time with conversation. Gradually the climate improved; after the second night, the landscape became practically tropical: palm trees, bougainvillaea, papayas, and above all, sun. In Canton it's between 15 and 30 degrees during the day, just on the nice side but certainly not hot. I had expected the temperature to be different! Hong Kong is three hours by train from here, so it won't be warmer there. When you go out in the evening, you definitely need a warm sweater. We are staying in a large hotel on the Pearl River, on the 10th floor with a lovely view out over the city. To my great joy, I got a letter from you right away, dated 26 November (the post takes so dreadfully long!). You write about how busy the town was for St Nicholas, while for me, St Nicholas (which we didn't celebrate, of course) is already a distant memory – let alone for you when you get this letter. I hope that the post is quicker when we get to Hong Kong, but I'm afraid that it will always take around five days. I wrote to both Mam and De Boer from Hangzhou, and I will soon send them another card when I've arrived in Hong Kong.

The domestic travails of their best friends, Kitty and San Go, who were being visited by San's elder brother from Indonesia, led Erik to reflect on the Chinese family system:

So Kitty's full of the visit from Djoen and spouse? After my journey to China and having had countless discussions about family relations, I believe that I'm beginning to understand this aspect better. It's incredible how much still lives on, even in the Communist system (which, after all, is in principle opposed to family cliques) – let alone in the *huaqiao* community. Kitty will have to be very strong to resist this power, and I don't believe for a moment that San is more 'emancipated' than any other *huaqiao*. It's completely ingrained, to the extent that they don't even notice it themselves. What has disappeared, perhaps (at least in some circles), are the external manifestations: kneeling in front of one's parents, wearing mourning attire when family members pass away, and so on. But the spirit is still 100 per cent alive, even here. Don't think for a moment that San will actually be able to extract himself from his elder brother's authority – I, for one, don't believe it will happen as long as Djoen is so close to Leiden. Kitty must simply hope that Djoen soon finds a practice (or a job at a hospital) somewhere in a distant province. For I believe that the current situation puts San in a hopeless (by Chinese standards) conflict situation. In fact, for him it is little less than a choice between East and West. Because in Chinese eyes, he must put his elder brother above his wife 100 per cent, and in Western eyes he shouldn't hesitate to give up his older brother for his wife. Once again: as a Westerner, it's very hard to imagine what 'family' means to the Chinese.

I'm afraid that I won't be able to come home directly from Canton. Hong Kong and Japan also need to be done; but the holiday in Egypt is slowly coming into sight, and then all the suffering will be over. After three months, I'm also starting to get tired of travelling. I'm no longer able to observe and record things easily; I've had enough, and I'm revolted by museums and exhibitions, having been to thirty or so of them…

This is also evident from the diary. His walks around Canton are described very briefly, by his standards, and a trip to a nature reserve (on the initiative of the guide) didn't go well at all.

Sunday 13 December
In the afternoon wandered around (great poverty, houses built in Mediterranean style, perhaps Portuguese influence from Macao? Very few real Chinese-style houses). People are more boisterous than in the North, and have a greater tendency to argue; southern mentality ('yes', *shi*, thus here = 'si').

Great that Schöffer's[141] book on the revolution has been published; the fee certainly don't amount to much, did it? Still, I'm glad that you're busy with your ladies' circle again. Not only so you have a focus, but also because it will get you more involved in university life. For I do believe that is fundamentally necessary – we're all in the same boat and have to sail together, even if some of the fellow passengers are less pleasant than we'd like. But the worst ones of all, like De Jong, we'll throw overboard! By the way, would you keep me up to date with possible speculation about De Jong's successor? (I'm sure you'll get a regular dose of the gossip.)

You asked what we knew about international affairs – and the answer is, nothing! Due to the massive demonstrations in Shanghai and elsewhere, we heard about the Belgian-American intervention in Congo, although there was no word, of course, of the 4,000 Europeans who were massacred (though I'm not tempted to shed tears for them; 90 per cent of them were undoubtedly mercenary scum hired by Tshombe). Otherwise, though, we have no news at all; in that respect, we're living in a vacuum. Luckily, that will come to an end in nine days from now, because we've had quite enough and are craving readable newspapers. In any case, this will do; three months in China is enough, at least if you do it in the extremely intensive way that we have done.

Be sure to go to the neighbours' for New Year's; they deserve it, and what's more, it will be more fun than going to San's house, crammed with children and family from the tropics. We'll be celebrating in the tropics; at least, we'll watch others celebrating. We won't be doing anything ourselves, of course; I don't know anyone in Hong Kong, and what's more, it would make me feel so disillusioned that I'd limit myself just to a drink. Concerning mink in Peking: there is indeed a lot of fur around. But in the first place,

141 Ivo Schöffer, Professor of Dutch History in Leiden. The book is: Z.R. Dittrich, *Zeven Revoluties* [*Seven Revolutions*], Amsterdam, 1964.

this mink (according to Tek, who knows about these things) is wild mink from Mongolia (not farmed) and thus of a much lower quality; and second, the pelts are not obtained in the right season, and are of mixed quality. There are also many sorts and price brackets here; in Peking I saw fur coats priced at 5,000 guilders hanging next to sheepskins for three tenners.

We're sending a crate from Canton with the last of the things we've bought (also mine), to be sent to the Museum (to avoid paying customs duties). We'll have to be very careful when buying things in Hong Kong; it seems one can be conned there in the most elaborate way; even Tek is hesitant about buying porcelain, et cetera, there. We're going to Hong Kong on the 23rd and will reserve a hotel from Canton. As soon as I know the name and address, I will write to let you know. We'd like quite a simple hotel, preferably in Kowloon, which is more 'Chinese' than the over-populated island. Canton is not very interesting, and here and there one sees shocking poverty and misery – a true port city with grimy working-class neighbourhoods.

Oh yes, with regard to Egypt – sorry that I didn't answer your question. I am afraid that for an organized trip like that, one would be tied to fixed dates. And don't forget that then we wouldn't be able to visit Istanbul and Athens on the way back, and that would be a shame; it's not often that one's in that part of the world, and we'd already be (relatively) close. Let's treat ourselves to something special this time, we all deserve it! When I'm in Hong Kong I'll organize my own return journey via Egypt and will write to Intraned. We should make it an extra-special holiday, without tying ourselves to fixed travel schedules, fixed hotels and meals.

Dear Puck, we're entering the home stretch, and we're more than half way! Tomorrow is our wedding anniversary – did you remember?? I'll write again before I leave, and then from Hong Kong – Tek says hello. Keep your spirits up in this gloomy month, lots of love and kisses to you both, Eerft.

Letter 15: Guangzhou, 19 December

Dear Puck,

I'm writing again, even though it's not yet Sunday. I haven't yet received a second letter from you here, and the first letter from you that I received in Canton took around 16 days to get here! Tek got a letter from The Hague that had even taken 18 days. When I complained, we were told that all post comes via Peking; that is to say, a diversion of more than 3,000 kilometres, with various interruptions – it's like sending a letter from Amsterdam to Paris via Moscow and Teheran! I'm now writing in the expectation that you will get this letter after 31 December, and it would not amaze me if you were to get my next letter, which I shall write directly upon arrival in Hong Kong (23 December), even earlier than this one.

Whatever the case, from Hong Kong our correspondence should go more smoothly; I think that the letters should take no longer than a week. I still don't know what my address in Hong Kong will be; we gave the names of two hotels to Luxingshe, which will make the reservation. We'd prefer not to stay on the island itself; it's tiny, over-populated and largely anglicized. Kowloon, which is connected to the mainland, is more Chinese and thus more interesting for us. As soon as I hear what our address in Hong Kong will be, I will send you a cable; given all the bother with the post, I think that's the best option.

I just got your long letter dated 1 December, thank you so much! Now I'm back up to date and 'in touch', even if there is a delay of two weeks. And what lovely writing paper, with a winter landscape and stage coach. I can tell from your letter that you're unhappy and unsettled. Yes, it is a difficult time, particularly in this gloomy month of so-called holidays, for which you're not in the mood, of course! But keep up your spirits, Puck; when you get this letter, it will probably be New Year soon, and then just two months to count down. We must keep our eyes on the future. You <u>really</u> need not worry about me and my state of mind, alright? Identification with China and the Chinese would not only be undesirable, but also impossible for a sensible person. The way people live and think here is so totally different that any Western European who imagines that he can put himself in the position of a Chinese is simply deceiving himself. Of course I can do my best to understand how the people here think, but that is different. Concerning Peking: it's a splendid city, and my remarks were inspired only by enthusiasm. But it is still a <u>foreign</u> city; a world that is indeed beautiful and interesting, but it's not mine. I'd rather have Paris a hundred times more than Peking, and Europe a hundred times more than East Asia. And that's also right; a person should broaden his horizons, but he should not become uprooted. Overseas Chinese are truly uprooted; somebody like Tek hovers between Indonesia, Holland and China – three native countries, and I see how this makes him suffer. I don't know whether Tek will return to China one day, as you write; he himself thinks that he couldn't get used to this hard life again, and that's probably true. He would like to bring his parents (who are unable to tolerate life in Indonesia any more, due to the mud-slinging and the criminal gangs) to the Netherlands, but the Dutch authorities will not allow it. He is put out about this, but I think that one should see it from the point of view of the Dutch government, which can't be keen on the idea of admitting as immigrants two people in their seventies who can't speak the language and who don't have any source of income. It came as a relief to Tek when we discovered here in Canton – coincidentally, in fact – an 'Overseas Chinese settlement' on the edge of the city. You wouldn't believe your eyes! In the city, poverty in small teeming alleyways, and right next to it there's a kind of tropical park with white villas and model schools in hyper-modern style, nice apartment blocks and beautifully kept gardens. Tek spoke with a *huaqiao* from Jakarta who lives there. For 45,000 guilders you can get a substantial house and go and live there. If you have enough money, there's no need to work, but you can work if you want to. From the Chinese perspective, it's a great way of getting specialists *and* foreign currency into China, but how different they are from the rest of the population! This group is thus officially known as the 'national bourgeoisie'. Tek is thinking about getting his parents to China in this way.

Here in China, every professor (*and* his wife, and all white-collar workers, in fact) has to work at a factory or farm for at least five weeks a year, welding bolts or wheeling manure around. The way things are done here is excessive, but the people here also view the situation in Holland as truly pitiful. Don't people torture themselves with all kinds of stories! But we are bourgeois in a bourgeois society, and we have to go along with it. Individual resistance is useless.

Hasn't Erik-Jan got a fantastic school report! Six 'nines'[142] – I never achieved such a thing in all my life! Truly something to be proud of; I'll send him another postcard soon. I agree that it's a shame that I wasn't able to send a present for St Nicholas, but alas, that's just the way it is. It's possible to send books (although that's also tricky), but when it comes to anything else, in the first place you need an export licence that has to be obtained at a state office, in the second place you're not allowed to pack the thing yourself (it has to be done at an official dispatch office), and third, the packet has to be officially cleared through Dutch customs, for which you have to go to Rotterdam in person. So wait a little longer, and Erik-Jan will get his delayed present in Egypt! He must have enjoyed Aznavour – is he still at the top?[143]

Here one never hears any Western music, only Chinese styles and occasionally dreadful Chinese marching music with choral singing, Russian-style. Chinese music becomes pleasant in time, but you have to spend weeks getting used to it before you can appreciate it. Since the row with Russia, almost all Western cultural influences

---

142 Translator's note: the Dutch equivalent of six A-grades.
143 It's ironic to think that the French singer Charles Aznavour would hold a much-applauded farewell tour in 2014, fifty years later!

have been banned. Even old romantic composers such as Chopin and Verdi, who were popular here, disappeared from programmes a few years ago. People are incredibly isolated here, and the Chinese sense of identity is so strong that this doesn't trouble them. People are also not the slightest bit interested in what goes on in the West, also culturally, for example. They still imagine Western Europe as it was in the middle of the previous century: grim poverty, female and child labour, and the merciless exploitation of the masses by a handful of bloodthirsty capitalists. And people don't want to hear anything to the contrary.

I haven't received a letter from Frits about De Jong; I'm afraid that it might have been sent to the wrong address. I'm curious to hear what he has to say. With your letter, though, I did get a letter from my father (writing about his problems with his eye, about another upcoming pay round – it will all go wrong if they don't stop!), one from San (impersonal chitchat) and one from Kitty, in which she describes, among other things, how she was carried away by the romantic episodes from grandpa's oeuvre that you'd recommended, and how under their influence she had recited Heine in the dead of night, accompanied by San's rhythmic snores. I gather from my father's letter that it will soon be Jan's [Erik's half-brother's] birthday (the day before Christmas, the 25th?), which I'd forgotten to note down in my book; evidently a Freudian slip. I'll put a card in the post today, even though it won't arrive on time; it can be combined with Jeannet's birthday on 3? January.

So our stay in Canton is almost over. We have a useless and incredibly lazy guide here, who thought it necessary for our amusement to send us to a recreation area around 80 kilometres outside Canton; a lovely river and reservoir in the heart of wooded mountains, a bit like the Ardennes. It was peaceful, but really not for us; we were bored silly. We wandered around a bit, climbed the mountain and looked at the waterfall, and took a few photos; then we told him to take us back to Canton without delay.

Wednesday 16 December

Went to the office in the morning; everything crated up and checked. We'll take all our things with us tomorrow. Then to Wenquan (in Conghua district, 80 kilometres north-east of Canton). A 'holiday resort' with white hotel buildings by the river, wooded hills, sub-tropical and admittedly beautiful, but otherwise goddamn boring.

Thursday 17 December

Told the guide at breakfast that we wanted to return to Canton tomorrow, not Saturday. Then went out with the twerp Wang, had a nice walk along mountain paths and endless stone steps to the Baizhang shuipu waterfall. Stayed there for a bit. In the afternoon I walked along the river to some farmland (Tek's got tummy trouble; in bed). We're bored out of our minds.

Now we're back at the large hotel near the harbour, in the big noisy city; really Southern Chinese with small, dark lively people, and narrow streets with countless open-front shops and small businesses. Even here, it's striking how little used people are to foreigners; I frequently cause large crowds.

So we'll soon be off to Hong Kong, back to the world of transistor radios, Cadillacs and pleasure yachts (and paupers with TB and cholera). As soon as I'm there, I'll get working seriously on preparing our stay in Egypt: discuss options for the flight, perhaps write to Brugman,[144] et cetera. It'll all seem real and it will cheer me up. I'll also sort out and frame my slides, and so as to remind you what I look like (hadn't Erik-Jan forgotten?) I'll send a few slides to you

144 Jan Brugman (1923-2004) had been Professor of Arabic in Leiden since 1961, but he had also previously been a diplomat in Egypt.

there and then. That's not possible from here; sending photos involves an unbelievable amount of trouble.

As I wrote, I've bought a great many things here in China at reasonable prices. There are even really old things available for purchase here in Canton (not the very best quality, but that is simply unaffordable beyond China, and in China itself it is not available for export).

Tuesday 22 December

In the morning, went to the Exhibition Hall. From there, we were taken by Mr. Guo to an art export business (only for traders from the fair!) where there were lots of genuine antiques; I also went along in the afternoon. Hefty prices; evidently the purchasing centre for the Japanese and Hong Kong art trade. Took photos of Shang and Zhou bronzes (17,000 and 13,000 guilders) and lots of small Buddhist bronzes (prices ranging from HK$ 1,900 to 290). Otherwise lots of old porcelain, et cetera. Tantalus on our last day in China. I've got a headache and am clearly getting a cold, I feel dreadful. Packed at the hotel in the afternoon, rested in the evening.

We have just sent a large crate to the museum, addressed to Mr. Pott. He knows how to deal with customs clearance and will want to carry out the formalities for us. That would only be additional trouble for you, the journey to Rotterdam, et cetera, and the museum has extra facilities for imports.

I'll bring a few small, light things with me in my suitcase (which is still holding up) for 'immediate use' upon arrival; I will be able to get some of them from Pott's crate when I arrive, and some others, which were already sent from Peking, will have to wait until Tek's return in July. Every piece that I've bought is of high quality and either unavailable in the Netherlands or else dreadfully expensive. I have bought simple consumer items, but those tend to be very heavy or easily broken (stoneware, baskets) and thus difficult to transport. NB. will you send your measurements to me in Hong Kong, for the Shanghai Dress? In Peking I bought a long length of black damask (or something similar, with a woven pattern, top quality from the imperial era), but that would be more suitable for a stole or such-like. If you've got lots of money here, you can in fact buy the most precious things! Like anywhere, the shops are full of junk for tourists (mainly Chinese tourists), but here and there are some gems. I'll buy some more things in Hong Kong, but one has to be careful not to be taken for a ride. I'm told that one is cheated and robbed there at every step. To be on the safe side, I'm sending you a complete list of what I've bought in China (on the mainland), in case I lose mine. I'll write again soon from Hong Kong. Goodbye dear Pucky and Erik-Jan, keep your spirits up, lots of love and a kiss from Eerft.

Chinese visa stamps in the journal.

Letter 16: Hong Kong, Saturday 26 December

Dear Puck,

So here we are in Hong Kong, safe and sound after three months in Communist China, although crossing the border took some doing. That's because we lugged our purchases with us in a large crate weighing almost 100 kilos, and what's more, Tek had acquired a living 'pot-belly' bamboo – a rare variety – almost a metre tall, which he plans to take with him on his future wanderings and eventually bring to the Netherlands (although the thing is practically dead already). Our papers were inspected for ages, and it was mostly the jade – only some of which we'd declared – that attracted the interest of customs. But we were finally let through, forcing us to run, followed by sweaty porters swearing in Cantonese, to catch the train to Kowloon/Hong Kong.

And thus we're back in the 'free world'. For the time being, still bewildered by the hustle and bustle and the dynamics of Western life. Skyscrapers, traffic jams everywhere and shops that are bulging with wares, both Chinese and Western. 'Western'; that is to say, mostly American trash. Our longing for good Western newspapers was not rewarded; aside from two or three local newspapers of mediocre quality, there's nothing here in Western languages, not even *The Guardian* or *Le Monde*, let alone our *Handelsblad*, which I had been looking forward to. After China, the level of luxury here naturally feels overwhelming. In the working-class neighbourhoods the poverty is evident, but to be honest, it is less terrible than I had imagined. In that respect, Canton is at least as miserable. The only (but important!) difference may be that the paupers in Canton and elsewhere in Communist China have a reasonable chance of escaping that misery within a few decades, whereas here, poverty is an absolutely hopeless situation. Little is to be seen of the English upper classes. The population is 99 per cent Chinese, and very rarely does one see an Englishman walking around or driving. There are Chinese wares, including art and antiques, in abundance, but the price difference is really incredible. Quite often we've seen little pots or jade objects here in the shops that we recognize from China, and the prices are six to ten times higher. Four small jade cups, which I bought in Xi'an for less than fifteen guilders, here cost HK $ 100 (= around 60 guilders) each! Luckily, silk and brocade are reasonably priced, so once again: would you send me your measurements as soon as you can? There are various beautiful colours and patterns here, mainly in different shades of blue (for example, a very beautiful azure-like colour, almost like this paper, with a fine bamboo pattern), but ivory would also be good. Would you let me know asap which colour you would like? I'll wait to order until I know. I'm not buying any more porcelain, I've got enough already. There is jade here in abundance, and of the best quality, but the prices are astronomical; you can't get a good pendant with a modern setting for less than HK $ 6000, and brooches costing 10,000 dollars are not uncommon. I'm so glad that I bought my knickknacks in China. The jewellers, who swarm around here, are extremely skilled, but they are rascals. There are also excellent traditional Chinese goldsmiths, though, who produce splendid work quite cheaply, for example in filigree.

Luxingshe has put us up in a hotel run by Dutchmen, called the 'August Moon'. Not a bad hotel, our rooms are spacious, air-conditioned and furnished in modern style, HK $ 50 (around thirty guilders) each. But we have to make a transition, and the experiences in this hotel do not make it easy; for the atmosphere is quite vulgar. Lots of noisy and quasi-jovial businessmen with stories about how clever they are and how much can be made out of the Chinese. And also a Dutch manager of the 'slap on the back' and 'just call me Jan' type, which I can't stand. So we're going to relocate tomorrow, to the Golden Gate Hotel, Austin Road, Kowloon (Hong Kong), where we hope to be able to spend the remaining 3½ weeks. After arriving we soon realized that the 'August Moon' wasn't a great hotel, so I sent you a telegram yesterday in which I gave as a provisional address, 'Poste Restante, Kowloon Post Office'. Perhaps you've gone on holiday after all and you haven't seen the telegram yet, but for now, just write to the 'Golden Gate Hotel'. The post shouldn't take more than five or six days to get here.

After China, Hong Kong is oppressively small, no larger than the province of Gelderland. We're staying on the Kowloon peninsula, opposite the actual island of Hong Kong, which covers just a few square kilometres. The island is home to both the large business centre with its banks and expensive hotels (the Hilton skyscraper, among others.) and the old Chinese neighbourhoods with their narrow streets and unbelievable masses of people, little shops and stalls. Despite the poverty there are few real beggars, but there are countless shoe-shiners and there are still rickshaw coolies. Nevertheless, it doesn't seem advisable to take an evening stroll in such neighbourhoods, and in various places one sees notice boards warning against pickpockets. Tek has made a kind of money pouch for me out of an old handkerchief, and has sewn it firmly to the inside of my trousers, around fly-height. As I've got quite a lot of loose change with me, I'm walking around with a noticeable bulge in that very place – an embarrassing sight, but an unavoidable one.

The prices in the restaurants are on the high side, but not exorbitant. One can get a decent meal for a tenner, and we also eat in small Chinese restaurants (among other things, raw shellfish in soya, which are tastier than you'd think), which are very cheap. I want to have some money left over (the ZWO doesn't need to know that) to be able to buy something nice here; some silk, or a good suit, or a good jade ring to complete your 'set'. We have to get used to haggling and tipping!

What else should I tell you about Hong Kong? The weather is pleasant (around 22 degrees), often sunny, lots of sea breeze. Otherwise it's incredibly busy and business-like, a mix of hypermodern and medieval, very noisy and often banal. In the evenings, there's an ocean of electric lights and a wonderful crowd of very well-dressed Cantonese hurrying off to restaurants, bars, theatres and music halls. An incredible number of shops, mainly selling those products that are especially cheap in Hong Kong, of course. Unfortunately, these are just the things I don't need: precision instruments, radios, telescopes, made-to-measure shoes, leather bags, and so on. I imagine Japan's like this, too, and I have to say that I don't think much of it. China could sometimes be boring or too peaceful, but this business-like superficiality and mindless pleasure-seeking lies at the other extreme. There's no decent book or magazine to be found in the bookshops – evidently people mainly read comic strips and *Reader's Digest*. Chinese friendliness and courtesy are also hard to find. The faces are stern and in shops one is snapped at in a manner that wouldn't be acceptable even in Holland. Anyway, we'll make it through the month. After all, we've heard that there's always the possibility of getting a special 'permit' from Luxingshe for a short trip (maximum of five days) to Canton, for the 'normal' Luxingshe rate of sixty yuan per day. Perhaps we'll do that one time towards the end of our stay.

Christmas passed for us unobserved, in the midst of all the marvellous Anglo-Saxon Christmas commotion. And perhaps you're in Paris, or another wonderful place! Out of sheer homesickness, I searched the whole city here for a few French records (to play at the hotel), but zilch – not one to be found. Lots of Beatles, Rockers and whatever all that riff raff might be called. And now it's almost New Year, and we'll start counting down seriously! Due to the holidays, we've not contacted the Consul General yet, but we'll do that very soon; my ticket for the return journey via Japan and India should have arrived at his office in the meantime. In Canton I got your letters with a delay of around two weeks. I'm curious as to whether another letter is on its way, and if so, whether Luxingshe will forward it on to me.

So you see, dear Puck, Hong Kong is a bit of an anti-climax after China, and I will be glad when this phase of the journey is over, too. This is the kind of 'orient' that Frits adores, but I don't get it. In the

Henny and son in Cairo.

midst of all the glamour and the bustle, we're lonely and forsaken here. But we're keeping our spirits up, you and I. Luckily the neighbours are still being kind and welcoming to you. Did you celebrate the New Year at theirs? I'll send another nice card to Erik-Jan.

Goodbye Puck, keep your spirits up, and lots of love and all best wishes for the New Year to you both. Kisses from Eerft.

This is where the story ends. The letters from the rest of the journey, which, after three weeks in Hong Kong, would take Erik via Japan and India to Egypt (and finally, in March, back home), were not kept, and the diary had already ended on the 22ⁿᵈ in Guangzhou. After Hong Kong, Tek returned to the Netherlands via Indonesia in July 1965. The huge amount of porcelain, jade, opera costumes, scrolls, prints, statuettes and traditional objects that had been sent to the Netherlands in stages arrived safely and are now kept, out of the sight of visitors, in the depots of the National Museum of Ethnology in Leiden. Many objects, however, including a five-haired brush for tickling crickets, can be found in the catalogue as an enduring testament to Tek's insatiable passion for collecting. The fate of the pot-belly bamboo, on the other hand, is not known...